Power Maths

Year 5
Practice Book 5

White Rose Maths Edition

Draw 3 things that are in your classroom.

What 3D shapes can you find?

This book belongs to _____ .

My class is _____ .

Series editor: Tony Staneff

Lead author: Josh Lury

Consultants (first edition): Professor Liu Jian and Professor Zhang Dan

Author team (first edition): Liu Jian, Josh Lury, Catherine Casey, Belle Cottingham, Wei Huinv, Huang Lihua and Paul Wrangles

Contents

This looks like a good challenge!

It is time to do some practice!

How to use this book

How does this **Practice Book** work?

Use the **Textbook** first to learn how to solve this type of problem.

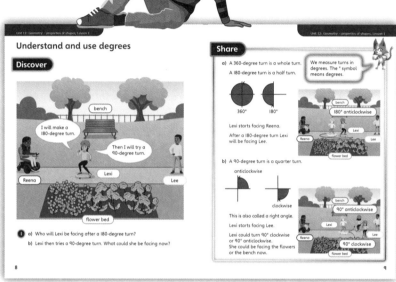

This shows you which **Textbook** page you need.

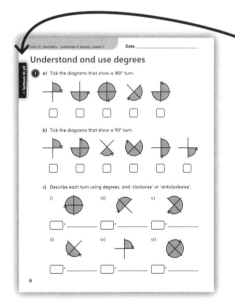

Have a go at questions by yourself using this **Practice Book**. Use what you have learnt.

Challenge questions make you think hard!

Questions with this light bulb make you think differently.

Reflect

Each lesson ends with a **Reflect** question so you can think about what you have learnt.

Use **My power points** at the back of this book to keep track of what you have learnt.

My journal

At the end of a unit your teacher will ask you to fill in **My journal**.

This will help you show how much you can do now that you have finished the unit.

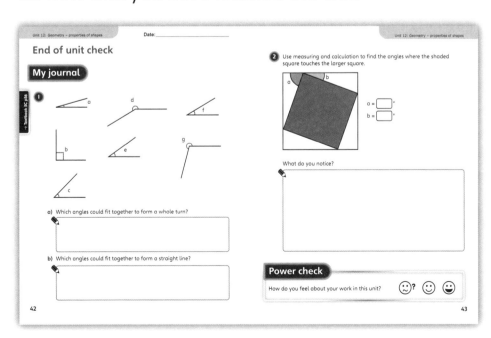

Date:_____

Understand and use degrees

1 **a)** Tick the diagrams that show a 180° turn.

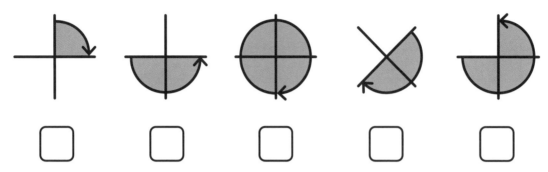

☐ ☐ ☐ ☐ ☐

b) Tick the diagrams that show a 90° turn.

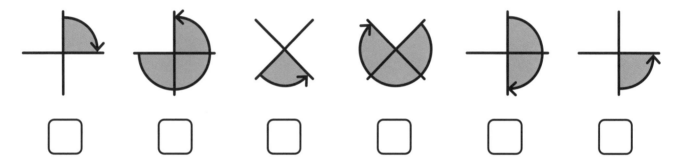

☐ ☐ ☐ ☐ ☐ ☐

c) Describe each turn using degrees, and 'clockwise' or 'anticlockwise'.

i)

☐° _____

iii)

☐° _____

v)

☐° _____

ii)

☐° _____

iv)

☐° _____

vi)

☐° _____

2 Complete the table for the different turns the ship makes.

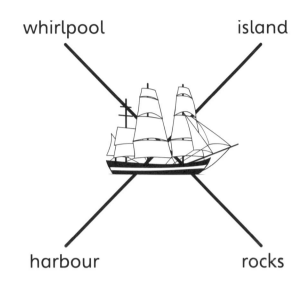

Starts facing	Turns	Now facing
whirlpool	90° clockwise	
harbour	180° clockwise	
island	[ ]° anticlockwise	rocks
	360°	island
	270° clockwise	whirlpool

3 Describe each turn in degrees, clockwise or anticlockwise.

a) Turn from B to F   [ ]° _____

b) Turn from H to B   [ ]° _____

c) Turn from C to D   [ ]° _____

d) Turn from D to A   [ ]° _____

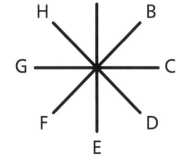

7

4 A robot has two buttons.

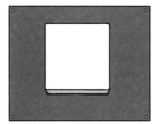

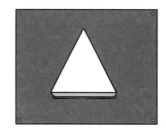

This button makes the robot turn 270° clockwise.

This button makes it turn 45° anticlockwise.

The robot is facing C and needs to face D.

Describe different combinations of button pushes you could use to make the robot complete this turn.

Which combination requires the fewest button pushes?

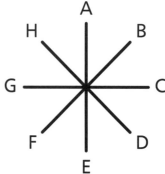

_____

_____

_____

_____

Reflect

Draw diagrams to show turns of 90°, 180°, 270° and 45°.

Measure acute angles

1 How many degrees is each angle?

a)

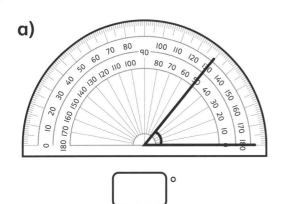

◻°

c)

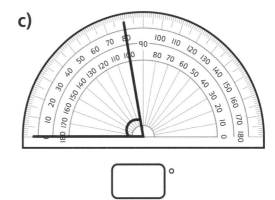

◻°

b)

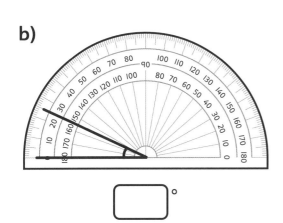

◻°

d)

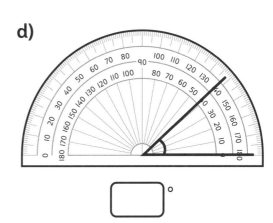

◻°

2 Measure each angle using a protractor.

a)

◻°

c)

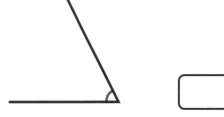

◻°

b)

◻°

d)

◻°

3 Measure the angles in these triangles.

a)

b)

4 Explain the mistakes Richard and Emma have made.

a)

Richard

This angle is 120°.

_____

_____

_____

b)

Emma

This angle is 40°.

_____

_____

_____

5 Isla says, 'I cannot measure these angles because some of the lines are too short.'

Find a way to measure these angles accurately and write the measurement beneath each angle.

CHALLENGE

a)

b)

c)

◻ °

◻ °

◻ °

Reflect

Explain the most important steps when measuring an angle with a protractor.

Date: _____

Measure angles up to 180°

1 Tick the protractors that have been placed correctly on the angles.

a)

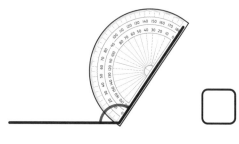

□

c)

□

b)

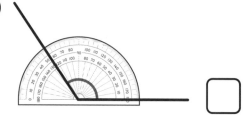

□

d)

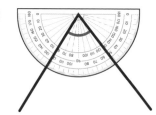

□

2 Measure these angles accurately using a protractor.

a)

□ °

c)

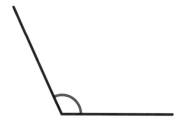

□ °

b)

□ °

d)

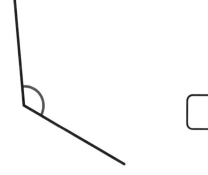

□ °

3 Put these angles in order, from greatest to smallest.

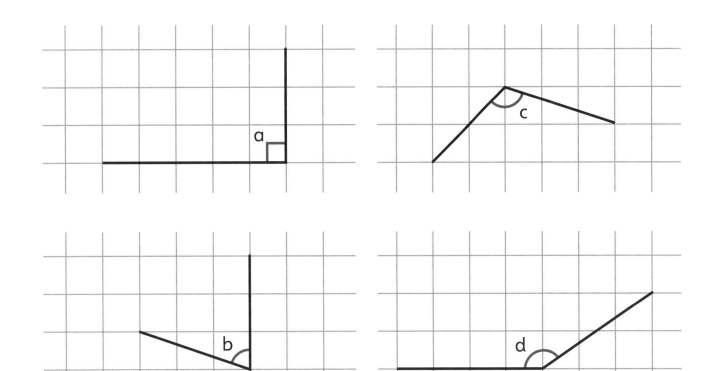

Greatest angle ⬜ ⬜ ⬜ ⬜ Smallest angle

4 Measure the obtuse angles in these shapes.

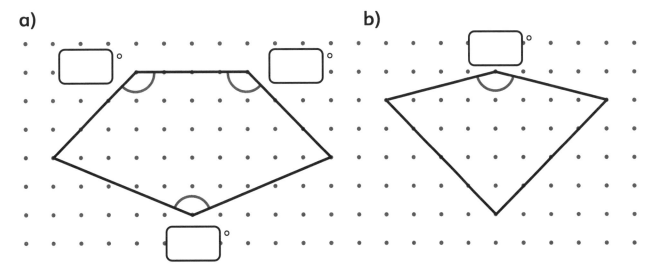

a)

b)

5 Max stands at marker X. He turns to face different markers.

Measure the angles he turns and complete the table.

CHALLENGE

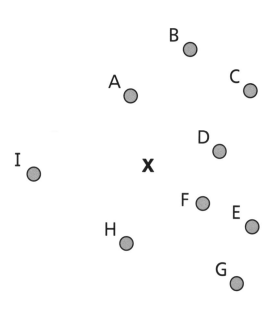

Turns clockwise from:	Angle of turn
A to F	
F to I	
I to B	
B to G	
G to I	

Reflect

How do you know which scale to read on a protractor when measuring an obtuse angle?

Draw lines and angles accurately

1 Complete the angles by adding another line.

a) Draw a 60° angle.

c) Draw a 30° angle.

_____

_____

b) Draw a 120° angle.

d) Draw a 90° angle.

2 Draw three different 45° angles.

3 Copy each step to complete the design below. Use your drawing to calculate the missing length and angles. Follow the steps using correct measurements.

The diagrams are not to scale.

Step 1

4·2 cm

4·2 cm   130°

Step 2

4·2 cm

130°   4·2 cm

Step 3

4·2 cm

130°   4·2 cm

Step 4

4·2 cm

130°   4·2 cm

?°   ?°

9·5 cm

The missing length is ⬜ cm.

The missing angles are ⬜° and ⬜°.

CHALLENGE

4   Draw a triangle with angles of 45°, 60° and 75°.

Are all of the sides the same length?

Reflect

With a partner, describe some common mistakes you can make when using a protractor.

Date:_____

Calculate angles around a point

1 Find the missing angles.

a)

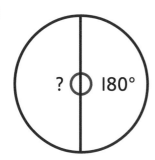

b)

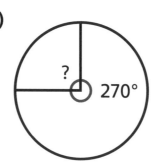

c)

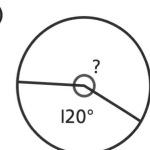

360° – ⬚° = ⬚°   360° – ⬚° = ⬚°   360° – ⬚° = ⬚°

2 Calculate the missing angles.

a)

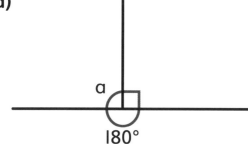

Angle a is ⬚°.

c)

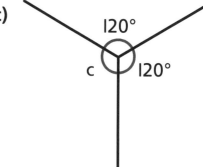

Angle c is ⬚°.

b)

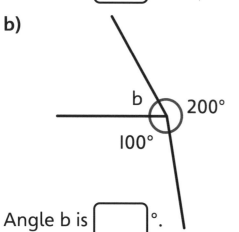

Angle b is ⬚°.

d)

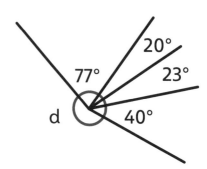

Angle d is ⬚°.

18

3 **a)** Draw an angle of 250°.

b) Draw an angle of 350°.

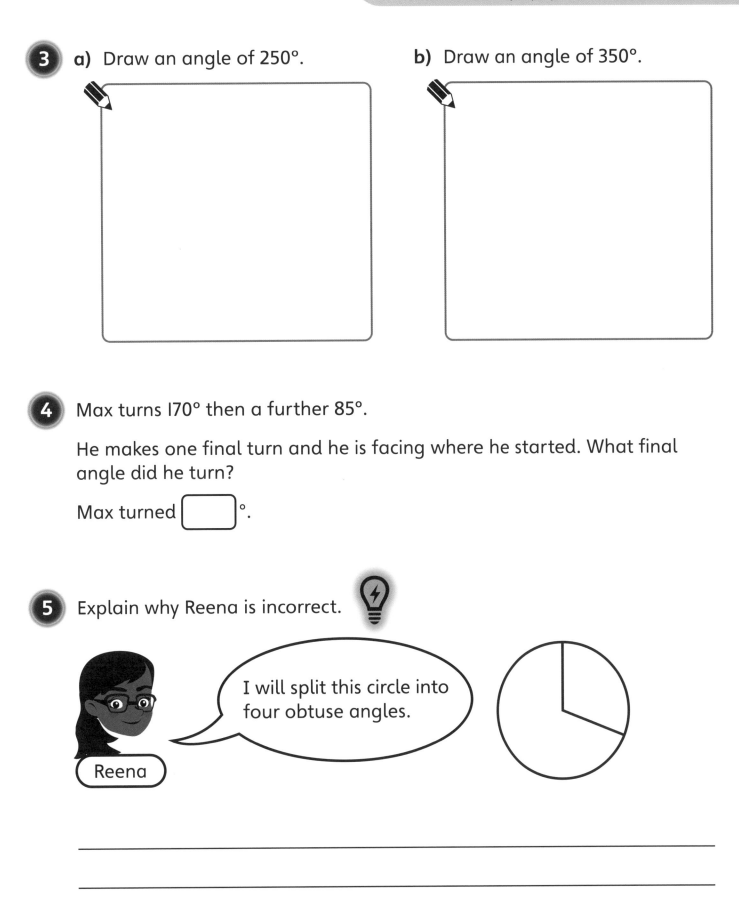

4 Max turns 170° then a further 85°.

He makes one final turn and he is facing where he started. What final angle did he turn?

Max turned ☐ °.

5 Explain why Reena is incorrect.

I will split this circle into four obtuse angles.

Reena

_____

_____

_____

6 These angles have been split into angles of equal size.

Find the size of each angle.

CHALLENGE

a)

b)

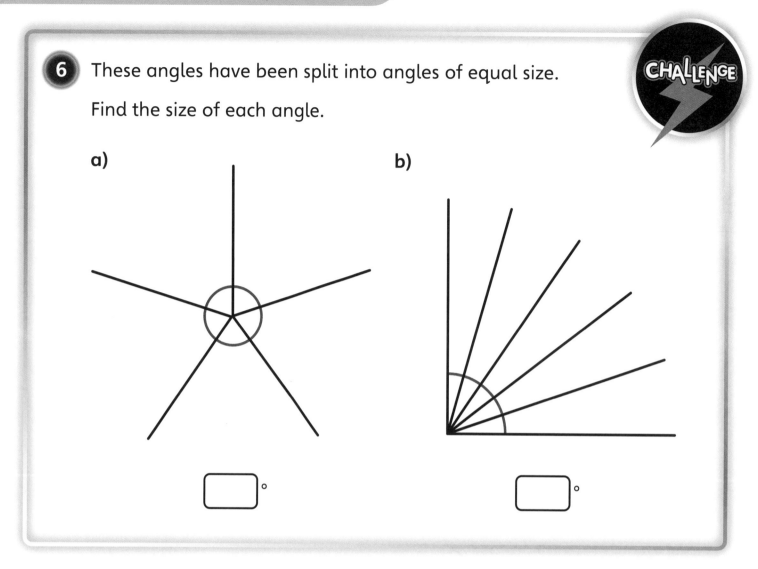

☐ °

☐ °

Reflect

There are three angles that make a whole turn. One of the angles is 110°.
What could the other two angles be?

Calculate angles on a straight line

1 Calculate the size of the missing angles, then measure to test your prediction.

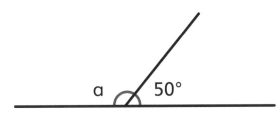 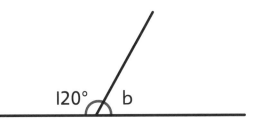

a) I predict a is ⬜° because 180 – ⬜ = ⬜ .

b) I predict b is ⬜° because 180 – ⬜ = ⬜ .

2 Calculate the missing angles.

a)

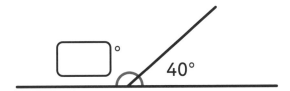

b)

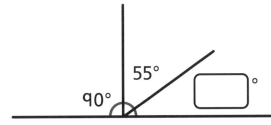

c)

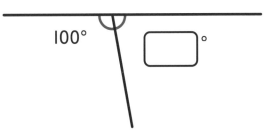

d)

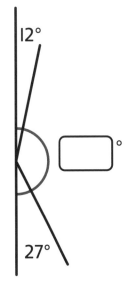

3 **a)** Find two pairs that join together to make a straight line.

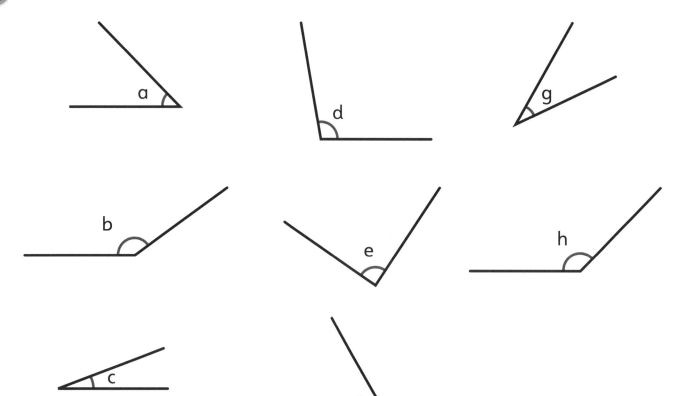

_____ and _____   _____ and _____

b) Find three angles that join together to make a straight line.

_____ , _____ and _____

4 Find the missing angles.

a)

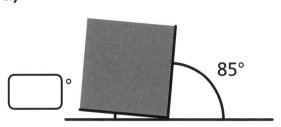

85°

b)

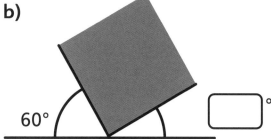

60°

5 All the angles labelled 'a' are of equal size. All the angles labelled 'b' are of equal size. All the angles labelled 'c' are of equal size.

Calculate the size of the angle labelled '?'.

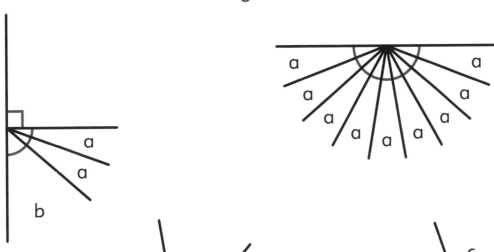

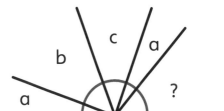

? = ☐ °

Reflect

Aki says, 'The missing angle must be 45°, because 45° + 45° is a right angle, then you just add on the other hundred.'

Explain Aki's mistake.

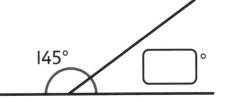

145°   ☐ °

Date: _____

Lengths and angles in shapes

1 Calculate the interior angles of each shape.

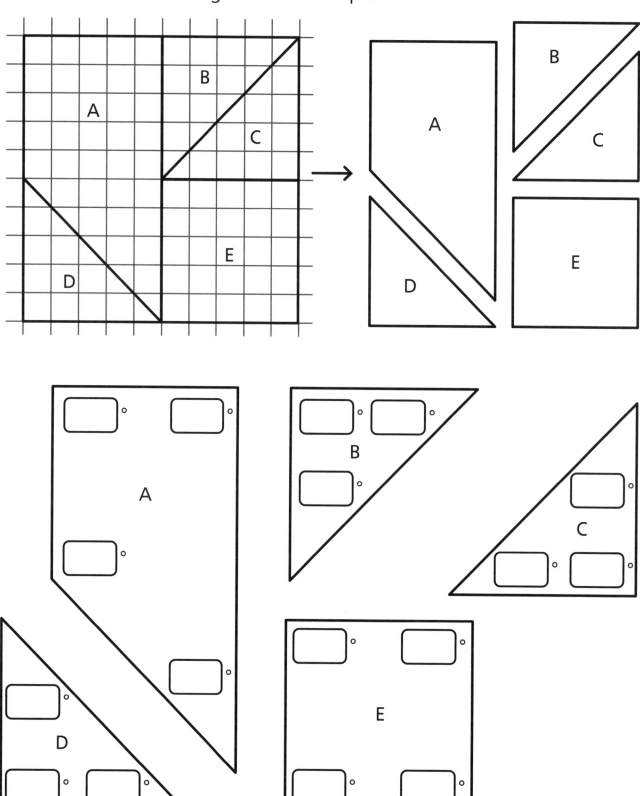

2 Find the missing lengths and the marked angles.

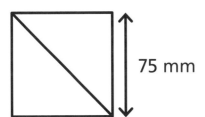

75 mm

a)

b)

c)

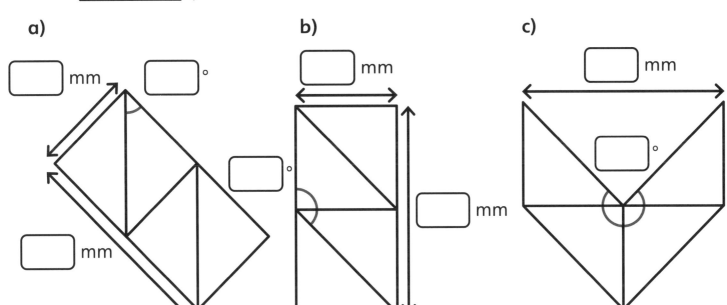

3 Calculate the missing angles.

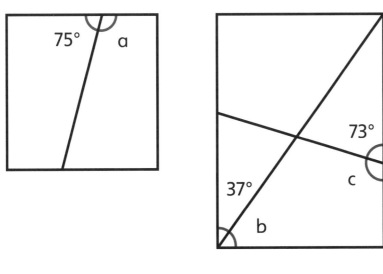

75°   a

73°

37°   c

b

a = ⬚°   b = ⬚°   c = ⬚°

4 The outline shape below is made up of six of these triangles.

Find the values of a, b and c.

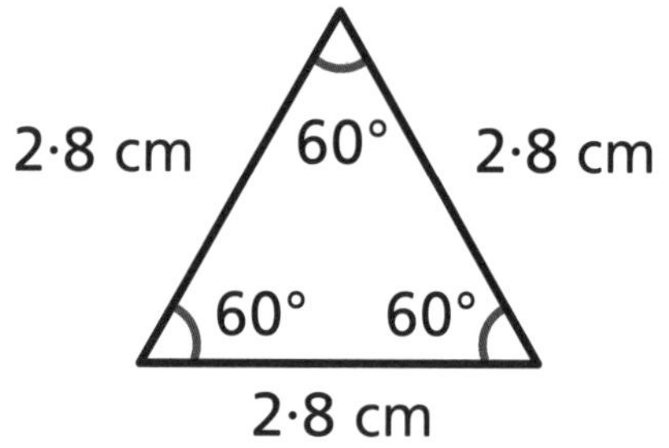

2·8 cm 60° 2·8 cm

60° 60°

2·8 cm

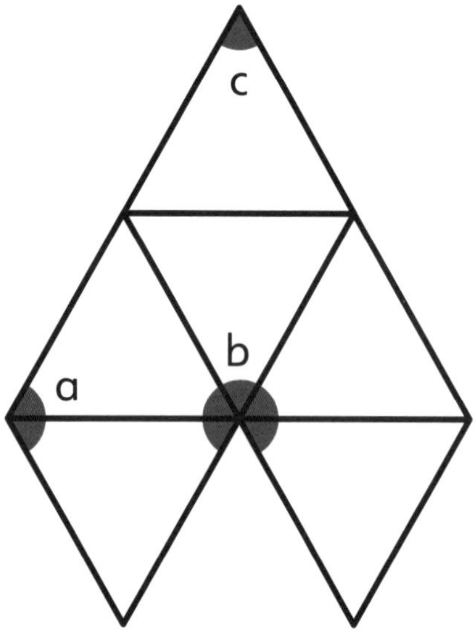

CHALLENGE

a = □ ° b = □ ° c = □ °

Reflect

'It is better to calculate than to measure missing angles.'

Do you agree with this statement? Explain your answer.

Date:_____

Regular and irregular polygons

1 Draw a line to match each shape with the correct description. Then circle the regular shape.

↓ Textbook 5C p36

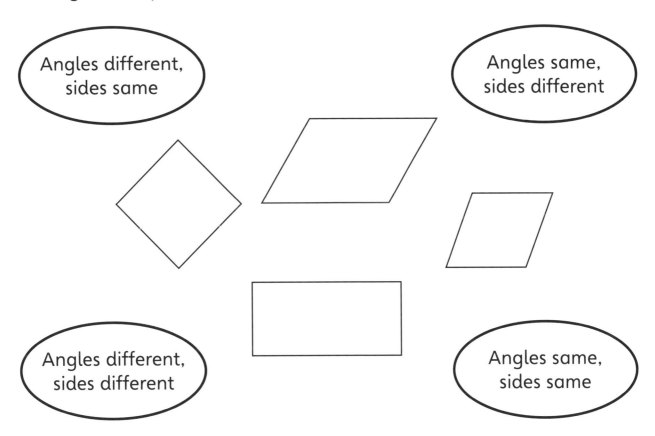

Angles different, sides same

Angles same, sides different

Angles different, sides different

Angles same, sides same

2 Look at the triangles below. Write irregular or regular for each one.

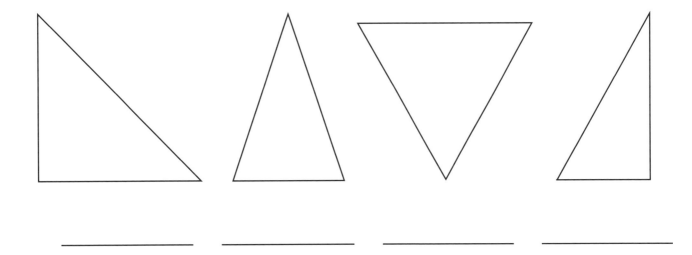

_____   _____   _____   _____

3 Explain the mistake Richard has made.

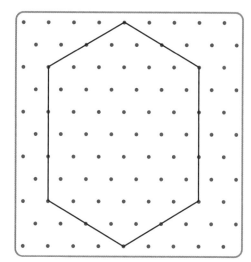

I have made a regular hexagon, because all of the angles are the same.

Richard

This is not a regular hexagon because _____

_____

_____ .

4 The shapes below are parts of a jigsaw puzzle.

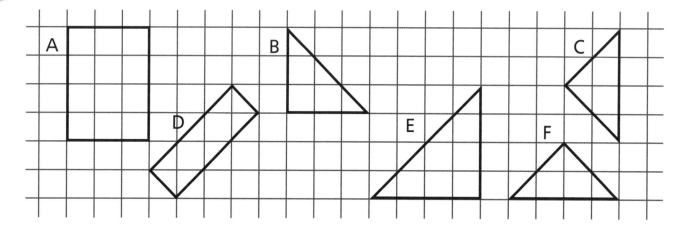

a) Which two shapes will join to make a regular shape?

_____ and _____

b) Which three shapes will join to make a regular shape?

_____ , _____ and _____

5 Draw copies of this triangle and join them together.

a) Make one regular shape and one irregular shape, using six copies of the triangle for **each** shape.

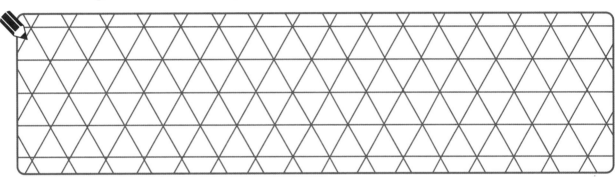

b) Make one regular and one irregular shape using four copies of the triangle for **each** shape.

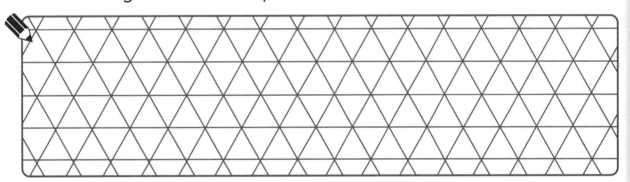

Reflect

Explain the different ways you can tell that a shape is irregular.

A shape is irregular if _____

_____

_____ .

Date:_____

Parallel lines

1 There are two pairs of parallel lines in each diagram. Mark the pairs of parallel lines with the signs < and <<.

a)

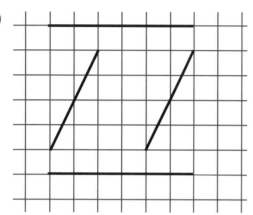

c)

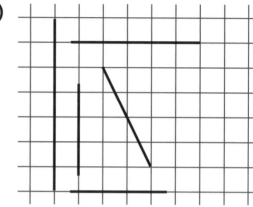

b)

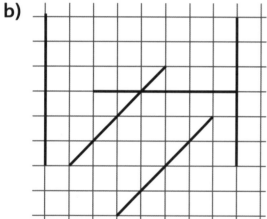

d)

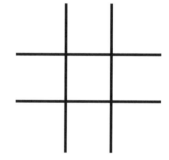

2 Mark the parallel lines on these shapes.

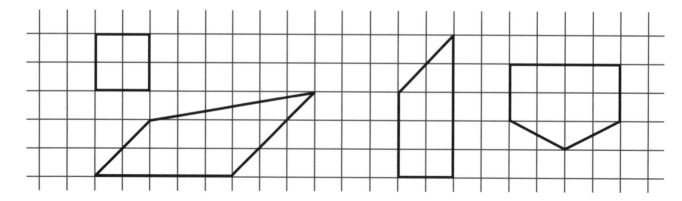

3 Draw two lines parallel to AB, two lines parallel to CD and two lines parallel to EF. The lines do not have to be the same length.

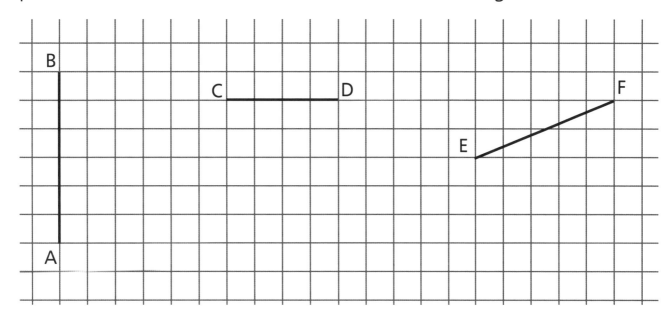

4 Complete the sentences about this shape, using the letters shown.

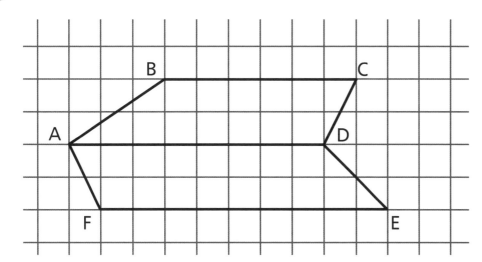

FE is parallel to _____ and _____.

Draw the line BF. It is parallel to _____.

Draw the line EC. Is it parallel to any lines in the shape?

_____

5   **a)** Complete the sentences.

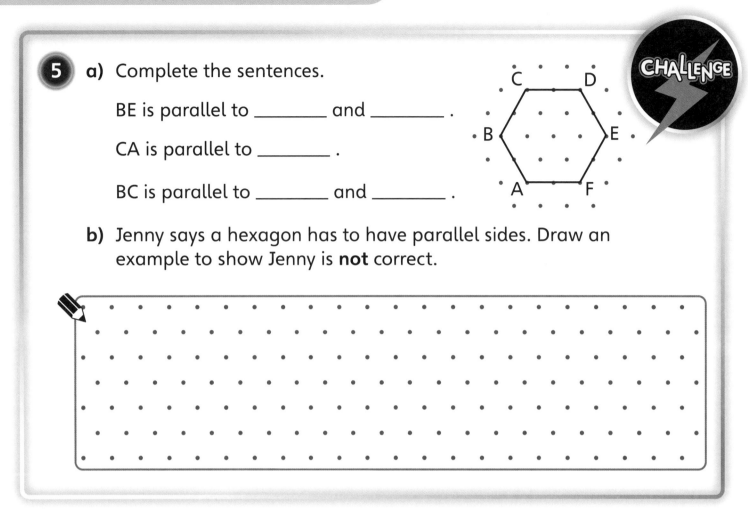

BE is parallel to _____ and _____ .

CA is parallel to _____ .

BC is parallel to _____ and _____ .

CHALLENGE

b) Jenny says a hexagon has to have parallel sides. Draw an example to show Jenny is **not** correct.

Reflect

Draw a shape with two pairs of parallel lines and mark them correctly. Explain how you made sure your lines are parallel.

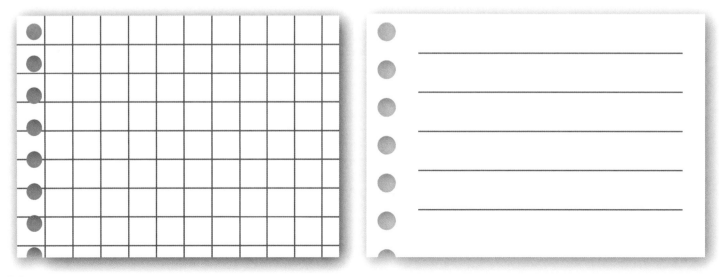

Perpendicular lines

1 Mark the right angles where the perpendicular lines meet.

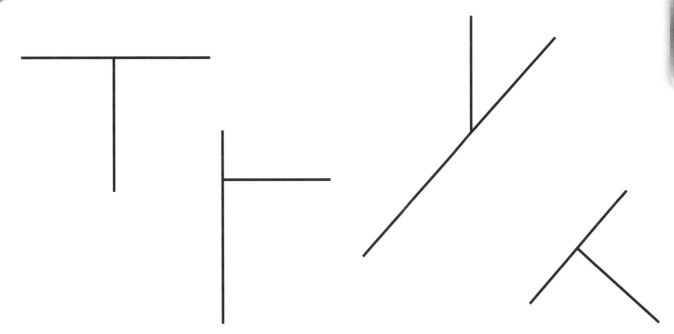

2 Draw a perpendicular line to each line below.

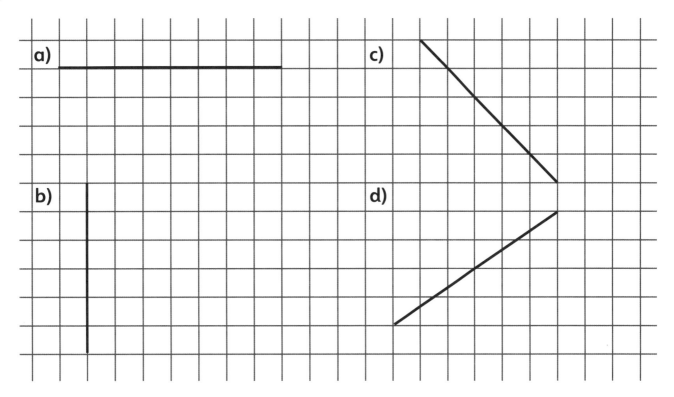

Textbook 5C p44

3 Mark any perpendicular lines in the shapes below.

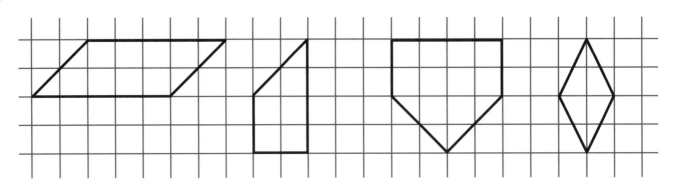

4 True or false? Circle the correct answer. Explain your answers.

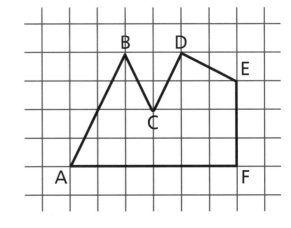

a) AB is perpendicular to BC.

True / False

_____

_____

b) DE is perpendicular to EF.

True / False

_____

c) There is one line perpendicular to AF.

True / False

_____

d) There are no lines perpendicular to DE.

True / False

_____

5 Draw a quadrilateral that matches one of the descriptions below.

- AB is perpendicular to BC.

- AD is perpendicular to CD.

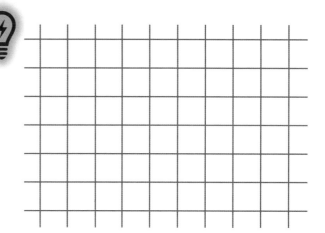

6 Draw two more lines to complete each rectangle below.

CHALLENGE

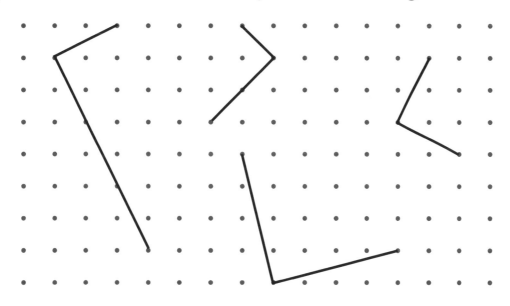

Reflect

Explain the difference between parallel and perpendicular.

_____

_____

_____

35

Date:_____

Investigate lines

1 **a)** Measure the angles below.

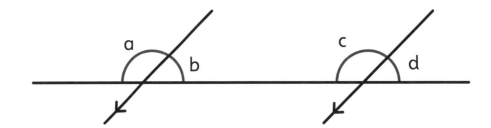

Angle a = ⬚ °

Angle b = ⬚ °

Angle c = ⬚ °

Angle d = ⬚ °

b) Explain what you notice about the lines.

The two diagonal lines are _____ .

They both cross the horizontal line at angles of ⬚ ° and ⬚ °.

2 Draw a line that crosses both the parallel lines below. Measure the angles and explain what you notice.

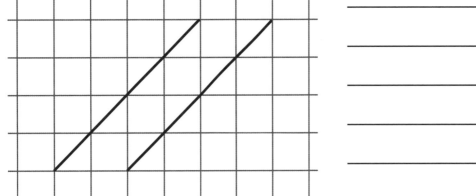

_____

_____

_____

_____

_____

3 The diagonals of quadrilaterals have been drawn below. Name each quadrilateral.

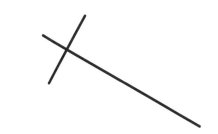

a) _____   c) _____

b) _____   d) _____

4 Do you think the diagonals of these quadrilaterals will cross at right angles? Draw the diagonals and measure and mark the angles.

a)

c)

b)
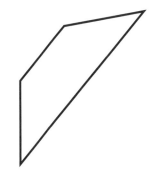

d)
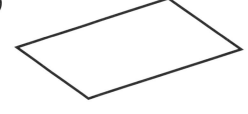

5 Join the dots to draw one parallel and one perpendicular line to each given line below.

CHALLENGE

Reflect

Explain how to fold a piece of paper so the folds make perpendicular lines.

Date:_____

3D shapes

1 Draw the face of the cube that each person sees.

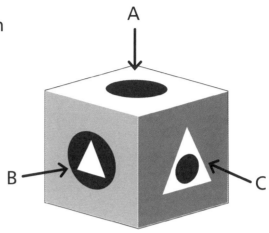

→ Textbook 5C p52

a) Person A sees:

b) Person B sees:

c) Person C sees:

2 Circle the possible views of each cuboid.

a)

 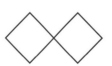

b)

  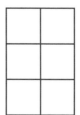 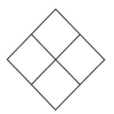

3 Three children look at the same 3D shape from different positions.

Isla sees a square, Aki sees a triangle and Jamilla sees a triangle.

Which shape could they be looking at?

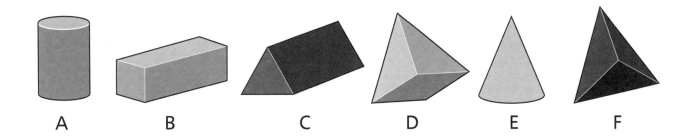

| A | B | C | D | E | F |

They could be looking at shape _____.

4 Draw what you would see from each different viewpoint.

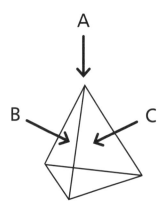

a) Person A sees:

b) Person B sees:

c) Person C sees:

5 Draw what you would see if you had a plan view of these shapes.

CHALLENGE

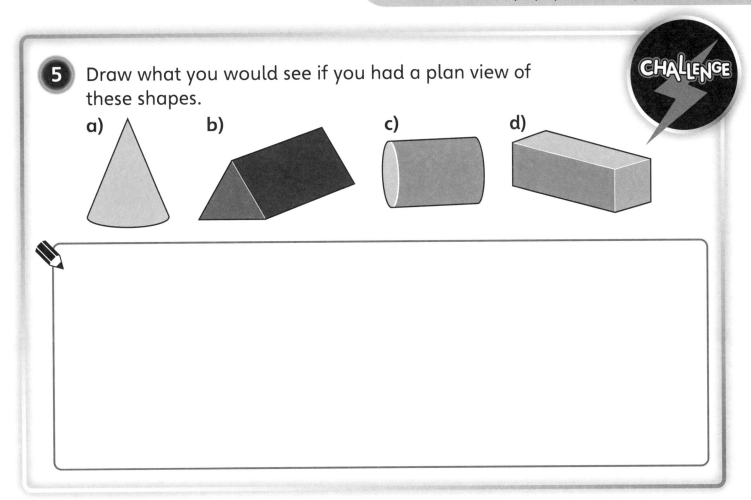

a) b) c) d)

Reflect

Draw three different views of a triangular prism.

Date:_____

End of unit check

My journal

↑ Textbook 5C p56

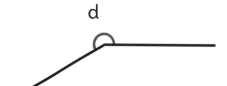

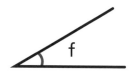

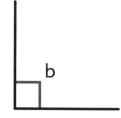

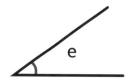

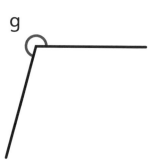

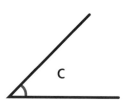

a) Which angles could fit together to form a whole turn?

b) Which angles could fit together to form a straight line?

2 Use measuring and calculation to find the angles where the shaded square touches the larger square.

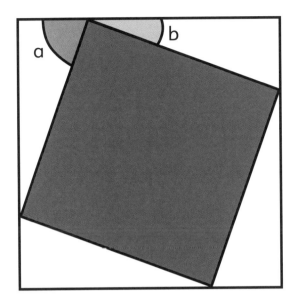

a = ☐ °

b = ☐ °

What do you notice?

Power check

How do you feel about your work in this unit?

 ?

Power puzzle

Use a ruler, protractor and sharp pencil to draw the star.

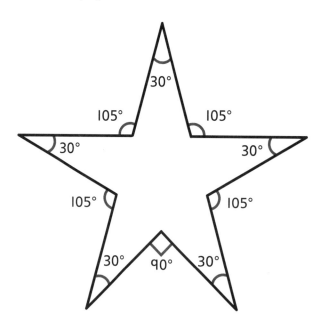

Decide how long to make each side of the star so that it can fit in the space below.

Make your own design of a geometric shape and label the angles. Challenge a partner to copy your design exactly.

Read and plot coordinates

1 Write the coordinates of each point. What do you notice?

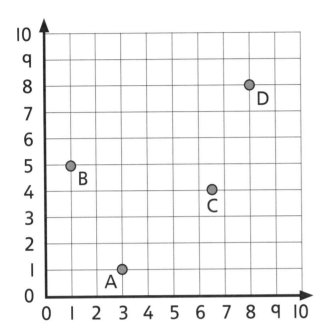

A(☐ , ☐)

B(☐ , ☐)

C(☐ , ☐)

D(☐ , ☐)

2 Mark a point at each coordinate.

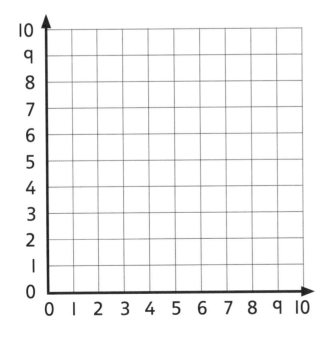

A(2,5)

B(2,8)

C(6,3)

D(6,6)

E(9,0)

F(9,10)

Textbook 5C p60

45

3 Draw a map of a mystery island.

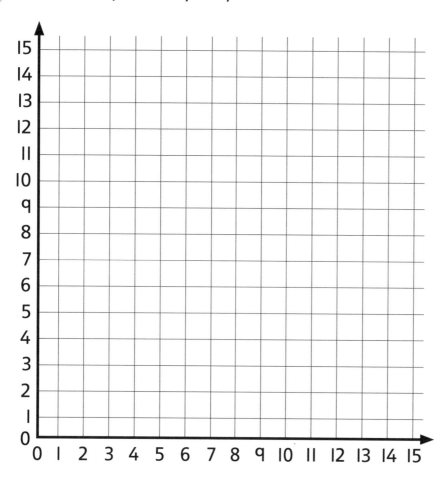

Use this key to mark important landmarks.

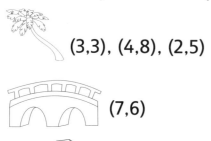 (3,3), (4,8), (2,5)

 (7,6)

 (5,5)

🌋 (☐,☐)

🚢 (☐,☐)

Add your own landmarks with their coordinates on your map.

CHALLENGE

4 **a)** Write the coordinates of each triangle.

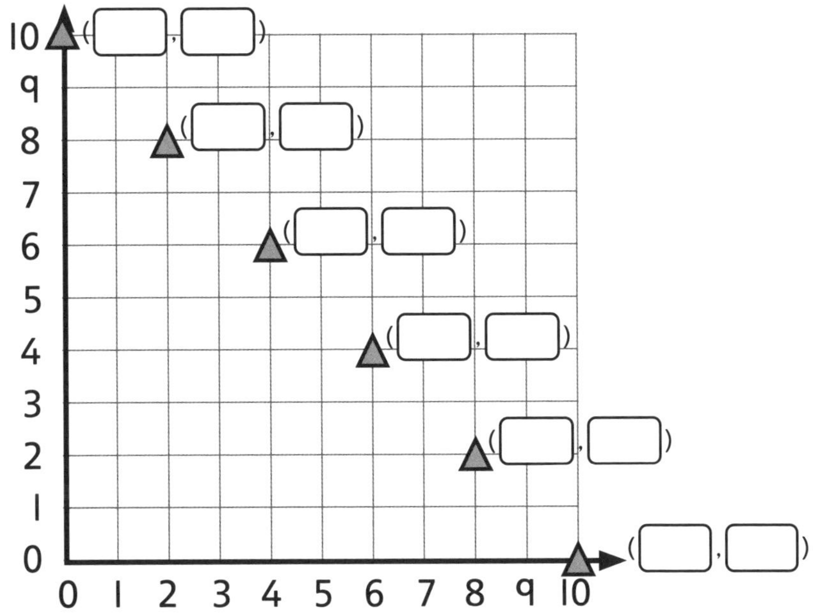

b) What do you notice?

_____

_____

_____

Reflect

How do you remember the correct way to write and read coordinates?

_____

_____

_____

Date:_____

Problem solving with coordinates

1 Two vertices of a rectangle are shown. Complete the rectangle.

Write the coordinates of all four vertices.

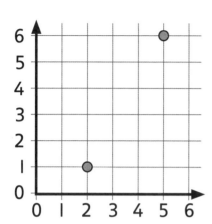

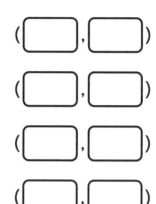

(⬚ , ⬚)

(⬚ , ⬚)

(⬚ , ⬚)

(⬚ , ⬚)

2 The coordinates of two vertices of a square are given.

Find two different ways to complete the square.

a)

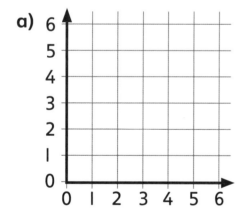

(2,3)

(4,3)

(⬚ , ⬚)

(⬚ , ⬚)

b)

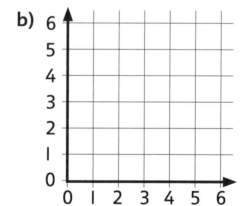

(2,3)

(4,3)

(⬚ , ⬚)

(⬚ , ⬚)

3 Here are three vertices of a parallelogram.

Complete the shape. Write in the coordinates of all four vertices.

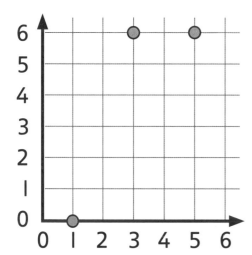

(⬚ , ⬚)

(⬚ , ⬚)

(⬚ , ⬚)

(⬚ , ⬚)

4 Work out the coordinates of the vertices of this rectangle.

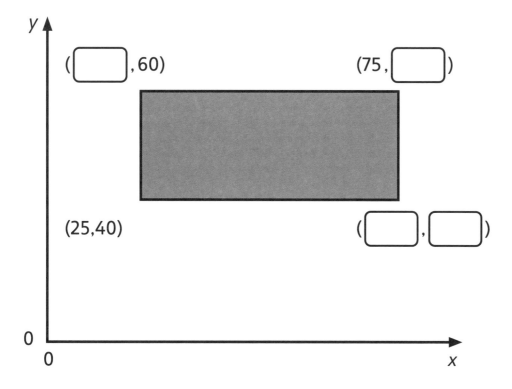

(⬚ , 60)   (75, ⬚)

(25, 40)   (⬚ , ⬚)

49

5 These triangles are identical. Complete all of the coordinates.

CHALLENGE

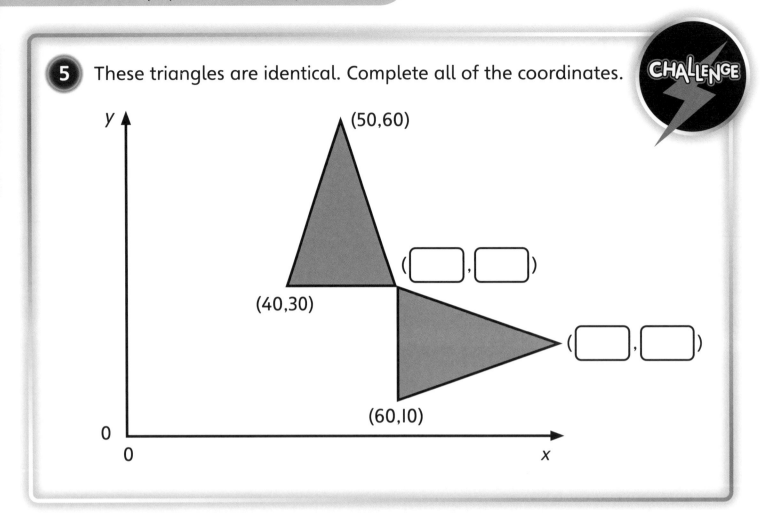

Reflect

Draw your own quadrilateral. Write all of the coordinates.
Think carefully about the properties of your shape.

Translate shapes

1 Complete the translations.

a) 4 right

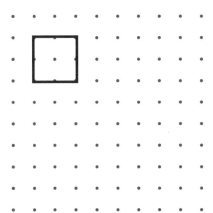

c) 4 left, 3 down

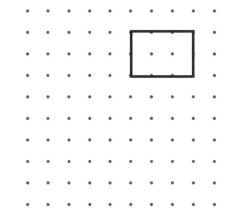

b) 5 down

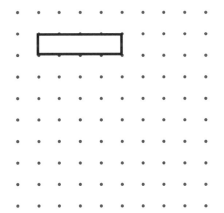

d) 6 right, 4 up

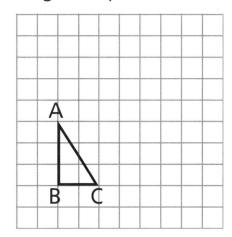

2 Describe the translation A to B.

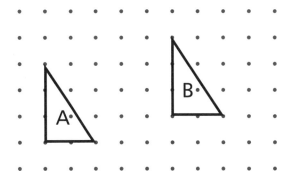

[ ] right, [ ] _____

3 A rectangle has been translated 3 right, 5 up.
Draw the rectangle in its original position.

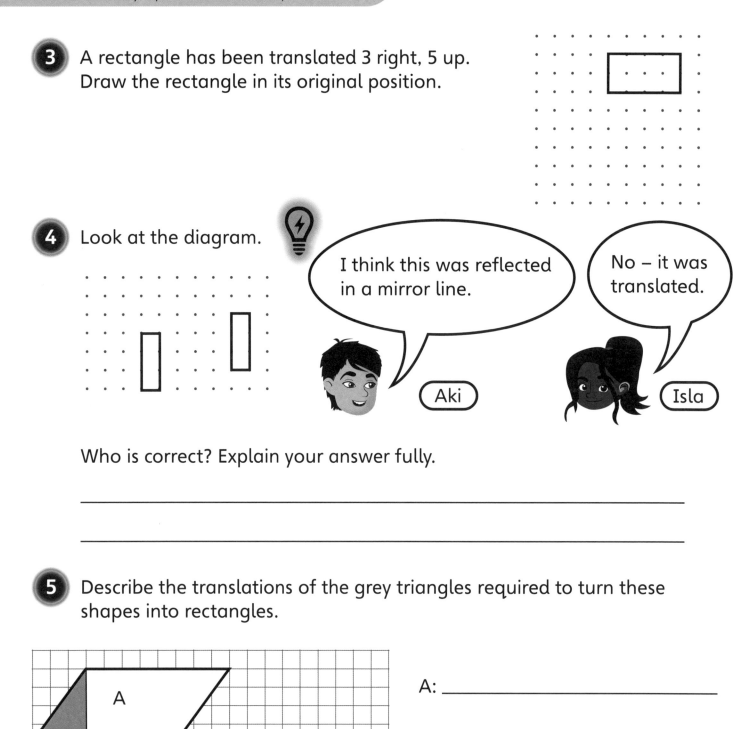

4 Look at the diagram.

I think this was reflected in a mirror line.

Aki

No – it was translated.

Isla

Who is correct? Explain your answer fully.

_____

_____

5 Describe the translations of the grey triangles required to turn these shapes into rectangles.

A

B

A: _____

_____

B: _____

_____

6 Describe the translations required to move the parts of the square to make the rocket shape.

CHALLENGE

B

A · · C

D

_____

_____

_____

_____

Reflect

A shape is translated 5 right and 4 down. Describe the translation that will return it to its original position.

_____

_____

_____

Date:_____

Translate points

1 The grid shows the starting position of points A, B and C.

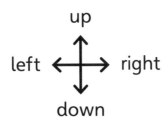

up

left ⟷ right

down

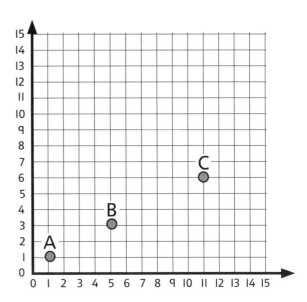

a) Perform the following translations in order and complete the table.

Translation	Position of point A	Position of point B	Position of point C
Starting position	(1,1)	(5,3)	(11,6)
3 right	(4,1)		
4 left	(0,1)		
8 up			
2 down			
5 right, 4 down			
Ending position	(4,10)		

b) Write the translation that goes directly from the starting position to the ending position.

Translation: _____

2 The rectangle is translated 20 right and 10 up. Write the coordinates of each vertex and draw the rectangle in its new position as accurately as you can.

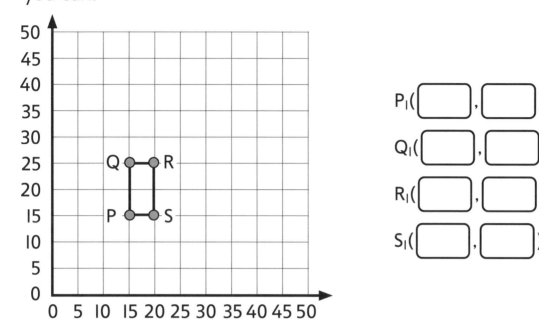

P₁([　] , [　])

Q₁([　] , [　])

R₁([　] , [　])

S₁([　] , [　])

3 A triangle has vertices at (4,4), (10,5) and (11,10). After a translation, one vertex is at (10,6).

What translations could have been made?

Find three solutions, and write the coordinates of the other vertices for each solution.

Solution 1

Translation:

[　] _____ ,

[　] _____

Vertices are:

(10,6)

([　] , [　])

([　] , [　])

Solution 2

Translation:

[　] _____ ,

[　] _____

Vertices are:

(10,6)

([　] , [　])

([　] , [　])

Solution 3

Translation:

[　] _____ ,

[　] _____

Vertices are:

(10,6)

([　] , [　])

([　] , [　])

4 Triangle A is translated and then reflected in the mirror line to form triangle B. Triangle B has vertices (14,25), (14,20) and (7,20).

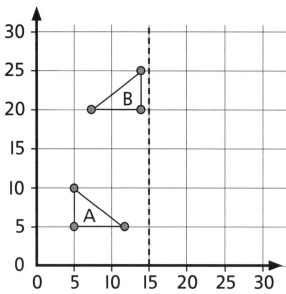

Work out what the translation is.

_____

_____

_____

Reflect

Discuss with a partner how to translate this shape on the grid.

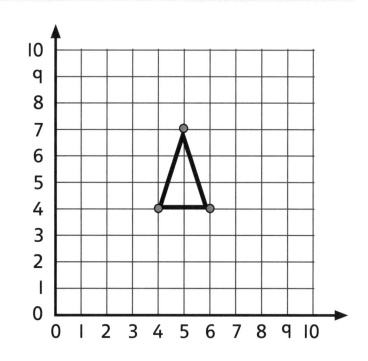

Date:_____

Reflection

1 Reflect each shape in the mirror line.

a)
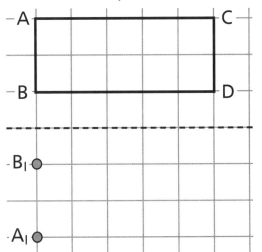

c)
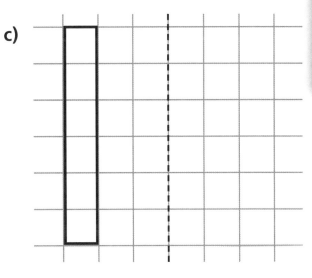

b)
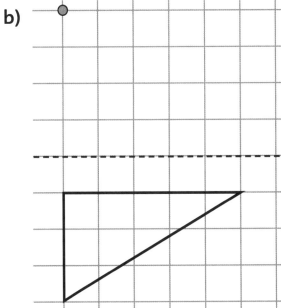

d)
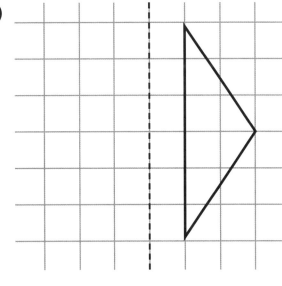

e)
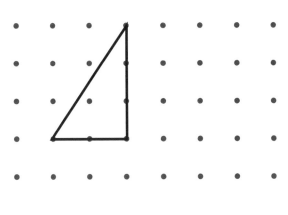

2 Predict what the reflected numbers will look like. Then check by drawing each reflection.

a) I predict that the reflected shape will look like _____

_____ .

b) I predict that the reflected shape will look like _____

_____ .

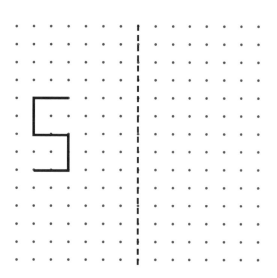
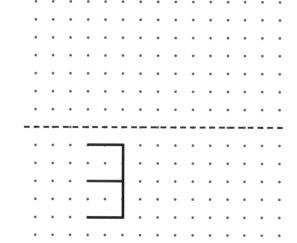

3 Draw a mirror line in the correct position between each pair of shapes.

a)

c)

d)

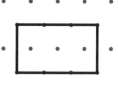

b)

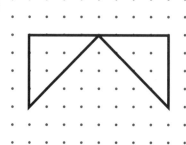

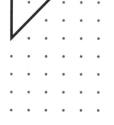

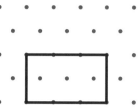

4 Draw each reflection.

CHALLENGE

a)

b)

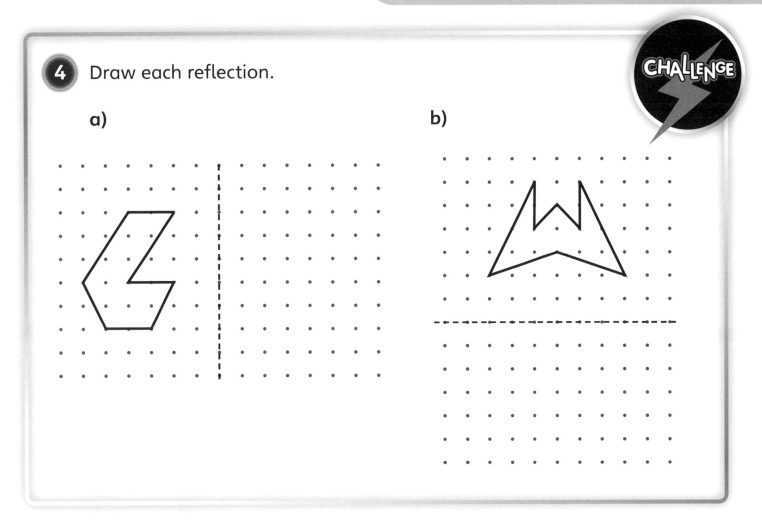

Reflect

Explain what will happen to the arrow when it is reflected in the mirror line.

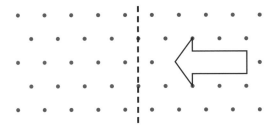

_____

_____

_____

Date:_____

Reflection in horizontal and vertical lines

1 The points A to F are reflected in the mirror line.

Write the coordinates of each point and its reflected point.

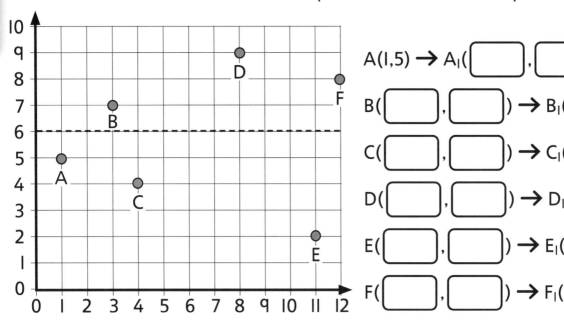

A(1,5) → A₁(⬚ , ⬚)

B(⬚ , ⬚) → B₁(⬚ , ⬚)

C(⬚ , ⬚) → C₁(⬚ , ⬚)

D(⬚ , ⬚) → D₁(⬚ , ⬚)

E(⬚ , ⬚) → E₁(⬚ , ⬚)

F(⬚ , ⬚) → F₁(⬚ , ⬚)

2 a) A rectangle has vertices P(5,1), Q(7,1), R(5,4) and S(7,4).

Draw the rectangle and reflect it in the mirror line.

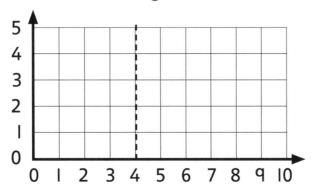

b) Write the coordinates of the reflected vertices.

P₁(⬚ , ⬚)

Q₁(⬚ , ⬚)

R₁(⬚ , ⬚)

S₁(⬚ , ⬚)

3 Write the coordinates of the reflections of the points A, B and C.

A₁(▢ , ▢)

B₁(▢ , ▢)

C₁(▢ , ▢)

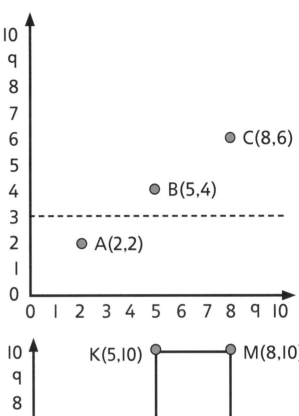

4 Write the coordinates of the reflected square.

J₁(▢ , ▢)

K₁(▢ , ▢)

L₁(▢ , ▢)

M₁(▢ , ▢)

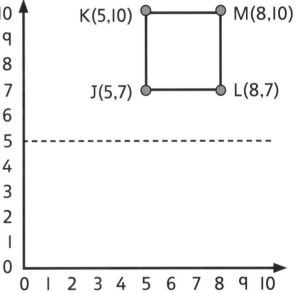

5 The triangle is reflected in the mirror line. Calculate the new coordinates and draw the reflection as accurately as possible.

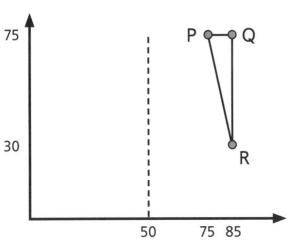

P₁(▢ , ▢)

Q₁(▢ , ▢)

R₁(▢ , ▢)

6 The square is reflected in the mirror line. Put one tick in each row of the table to show the correct position of each coordinate listed in the Point column.

CHALLENGE

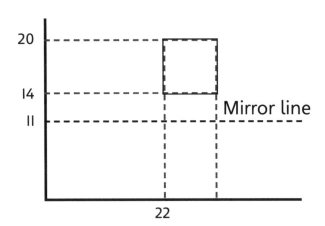

Mirror line

Point	Inside original square	Inside reflected square	Outside both squares
(23,21)			
(25,5)			
(29,5)			
(27,17)			
(20,7)			
(10,10)			

Reflect

Discuss with a partner how you can use coordinates to calculate the reflection of a point.

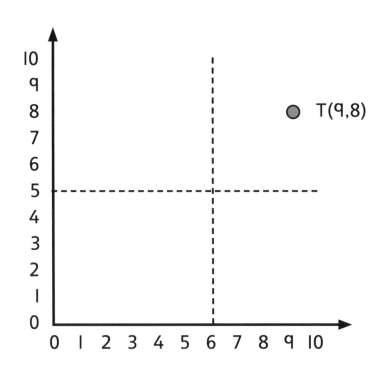

Date: _____

End of unit check

→ Textbook 5C p84

1 This parallelogram has been reflected in the mirror line.

What are the coordinates of the missing points A to E?

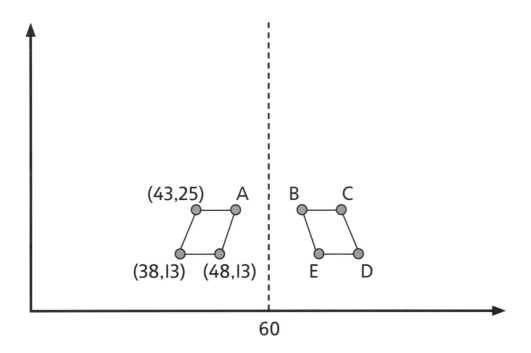

A(☐ , ☐)

B(☐ , ☐)

C(☐ , ☐)

D(☐ , ☐)

E(☐ , ☐)

2 The triangle has been reflected twice. Draw the two mirror lines.

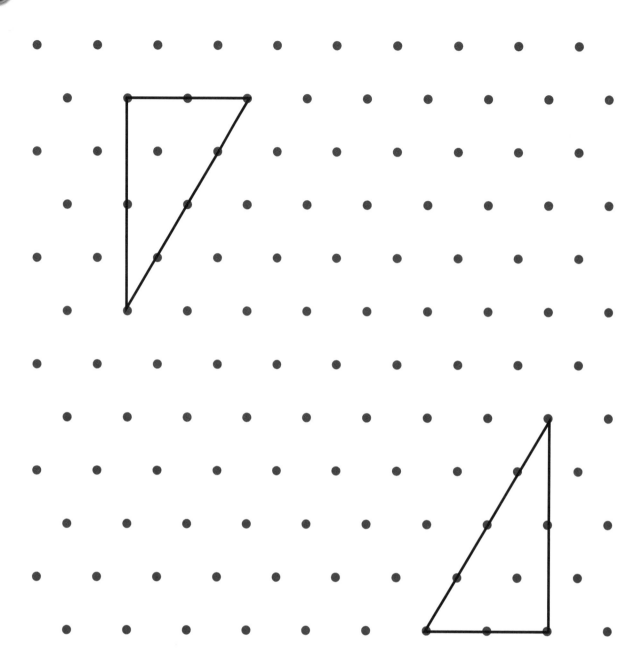

Power puzzle

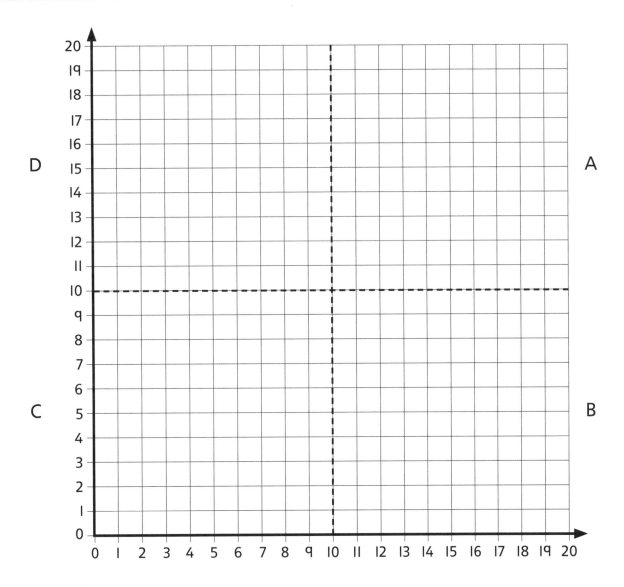

Draw a design in section A.

Reflect it in the mirror lines so you have four copies of your design.

What do you notice about the different shapes?

Try including diagonal lines, or using half-squares to make a complex symmetric pattern.

Date: _____

Add and subtract decimals within 1 ❶

① Find the totals of these decimals.

a) $0.4 + 0.5 =$ ⬚

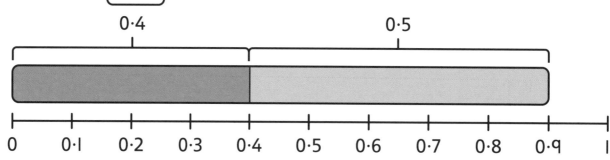

b) $0.7 + 0.1 =$ ⬚

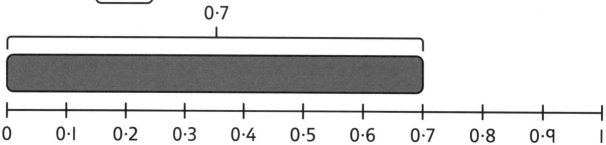

c) $0.3 + 0.1 + 0.3 =$ ⬚   **d)** $0.5 + 0.5 =$ ⬚

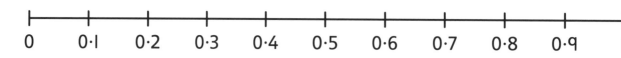

② Max cuts some pieces of string. He measures the lengths, which are in metres.

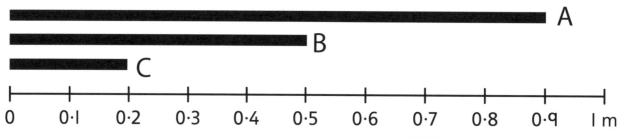

a) How much longer is A than B?   ⬚ – ⬚ = ⬚ m

b) What is the difference between A and C?   ⬚ – ⬚ = ⬚ m

3 Complete the part-whole models.

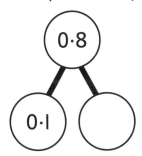 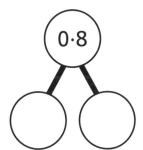 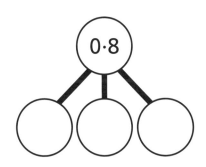

4 Complete the calculations.

a) $0.3 + 0.5 = \boxed{}$

b) $0.7 + 0.1 = \boxed{}$

c) $0.2 + \boxed{} = 0.5$

d) $0.5 - 0.1 = \boxed{}$

e) $0.8 - 0.2 = \boxed{}$

f) $0.7 - \boxed{} = 0.2$

g) $0.4 + 0.3 + 0.2 = \boxed{}$

h) $0.7 + 0.2 - 0.3 = \boxed{}$

i) $0.9 - 0.1 + 0.2 = \boxed{}$

j) $0.5 - 0.2 - 0.3 = \boxed{}$

5 Complete the following calculations.

a) $0.3 + 0.7 = \boxed{}$

b) $0.6 + \boxed{} = 1$

c) $\boxed{} + 0.1 = 1$

d) $1 - 0.2 = \boxed{}$

e) $1 - 0.5 = \boxed{}$

f) $1 - \boxed{} = 0.2$

6 Complete the addition pyramids. Each row of the pyramid must total the same as the other rows.

a)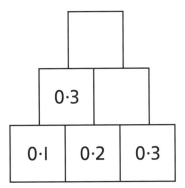

b)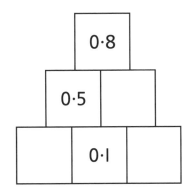

c)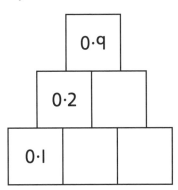

7 If ◆ and ▲ are two decimal numbers less than 1 and ▲ − ◆ = 0·3, what could ▲ and ◆ be?

8 Write the decimal numbers 0·1, 0·2, 0·3, 0·4, 0·5 and 0·6 in the circles so that the sum of each side of the triangle is equal to 0·9. Use each number once.

CHALLENGE

Reflect

Emma calculates 0·4 + 1 = 0·5. Explain the mistake Emma has made.

Add and subtract decimals within 1 ❷

1 Complete the additions.

a) 0·36 + 0·22

	O	•	Tth	Hth
	0	•	3	6
+	0	•	2	2
		•		

c) 0·55 + 0·31

	O	•	Tth	Hth
	0	•	5	5
+	0	•	3	1
		•		

b) 0·25 + 0·44

	O	•	Tth	Hth
	0	•	2	5
+	0	•	4	4
		•		

d) 0·34 + 0·34

	O	•	Tth	Hth
		•		
+		•		
		•		

2 Complete the part-whole model.

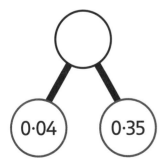

	O	•	Tth	Hth
		•		
+		•		
		•		

3 Complete the subtractions.

a) 0·99 − 0·58

	O	•Tth	Hth
	0	9	9
−	0	5	8

c) 0·75 − 0·24

	O	•Tth	Hth
	0	7	5
−	0	2	4

b) 0·49 − 0·19

	O	•Tth	Hth
	0	4	9
−	0	1	9

d) 0·49 − 0·45

	O	•Tth	Hth
−			

4 A running race is 0·65 km long.

Lee runs 0·34 km.

How far is left to run?

	O	•Tth	Hth
	0	6	5
−	0	3	4

5 Fill in the missing number.

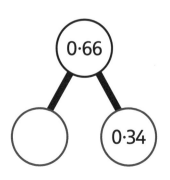

6 Max has some boxes.

The mass of each box is shown.

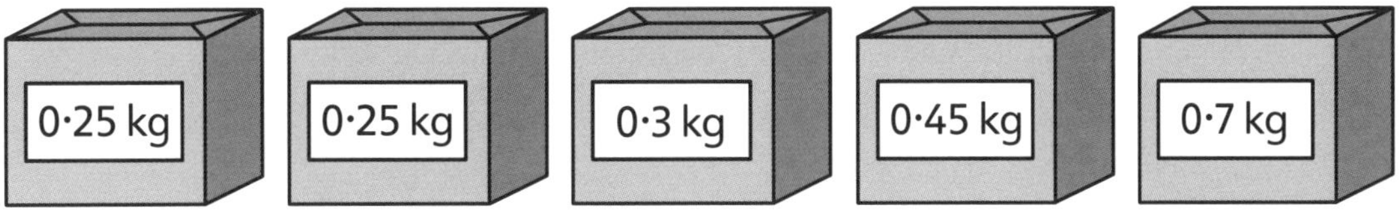

| 0·25 kg | 0·25 kg | 0·3 kg | 0·45 kg | 0·7 kg |

a) Which two boxes can balance these scales?

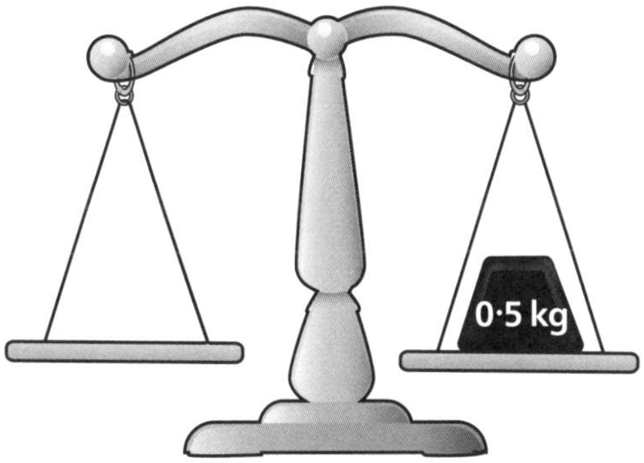

0·5 kg

b) Find two possible ways to add boxes to balance these scales.

1 kg

Reflect

Explain how Alex can use 32 + 16 to find the sum of 0·32 and 0·16.

Date: _____

Complements to 1

1 Use the grids to help you find the missing numbers.

a) 0·8 + [ ] = 1

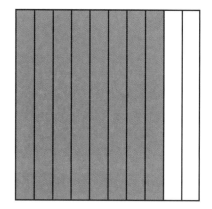

b) 0·69 + [ ] = 1

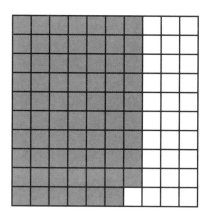

2 Draw lines to match the pairs that make 1 m when added together.

0·76 m	**0·88 m**
0·12 m	**0·24 m**
0·45 m	**0·234 m**
0·9 m	**0·55 m**
0·766 m	**0·1 m**

3 Lexi has made the number 0·26 on a place value grid.

O		Tth	Hth
		⓪·₁ ⓪·₁	⓪·₀₁ ⓪·₀₁ ⓪·₀₁ ⓪·₀₁ ⓪·₀₁ ⓪·₀₁

I need to add 0·84 to make 1.

What mistake has Lexi made?

Lexi

What counters does she need to add to make 1?

_____

_____

4 a) Find the missing numbers.

i)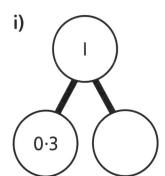

ii)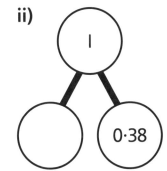

iii)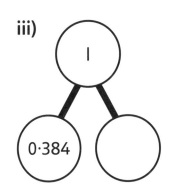

b) Complete the fact family for part ii) in a).

0·38 + ☐ = 1   ☐ + ☐ = 1

1 − ☐ = ☐   ☐ − ☐ = ☐

5 Complete the following.

a) 0·8 + ☐ = 1   d) 0·90 + ☐ = 1   g) 1 − 0·24 = ☐

b) 0·71 + ☐ = 1   e) ☐ + 0·78 = 1   h) 1 − ☐ = 0·07

c) ☐ + 0·05 = 1   f) 0·912 + ☐ = 1   i) 1 − 0·235 = ☐

6 Work out the missing numbers.

a)   0·4 + [ ] = 1

0·04 + [ ] = 1

0·004 + [ ] = 1

b)   0·4 + [ ] = 1

0·40 + [ ] = 1

0·400 + [ ] = 1

7 **a)** Use six digits from 1, 3, 4, 5, 7, 8 to make two decimal numbers that add up to 1. You can use the same digit more than once but not within the same number.

CHALLENGE

b) Find another answer for part a).

What is the same and what is different about your answers?

_____

_____

Reflect

Andy says, '0·207 + 0·793 = 1.' Do you agree? Explain your answer.

Add and subtract decimals across 1

1 Use the number lines to work out the following calculations.

a) $0.7 + 0.5 = \boxed{}$

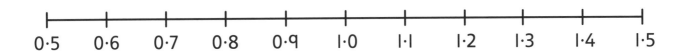

0.5 0.6 0.7 0.8 0.9 1.0 1.1 1.2 1.3 1.4 1.5

b) $0.8 + 0.7 = \boxed{}$

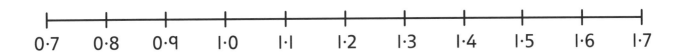

0.7 0.8 0.9 1.0 1.1 1.2 1.3 1.4 1.5 1.6 1.7

c) $1.5 + 0.9 = \boxed{}$

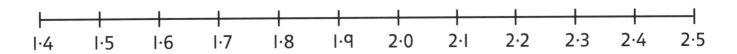

1.4 1.5 1.6 1.7 1.8 1.9 2.0 2.1 2.2 2.3 2.4 2.5

d) $1.2 - 0.8 = \boxed{}$

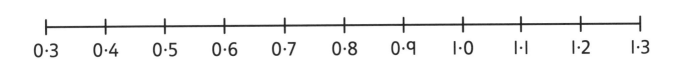

0.3 0.4 0.5 0.6 0.7 0.8 0.9 1.0 1.1 1.2 1.3

2 Complete the calculations.

a) $6 + 7 = \boxed{}$

$0{\cdot}6 + 0{\cdot}7 = \boxed{}$

$0{\cdot}06 + 0{\cdot}07 = \boxed{}$

$0{\cdot}006 + 0{\cdot}007 = \boxed{}$

b) $15 - 9 = \boxed{}$

$1{\cdot}5 - 0{\cdot}9 = \boxed{}$

$0{\cdot}15 - 0{\cdot}09 = \boxed{}$

Discuss with a partner any patterns you notice.

3 Work out the calculations.

Show how you worked out the answer on the number lines.

a) $2{\cdot}5 - 0{\cdot}7 = \boxed{}$

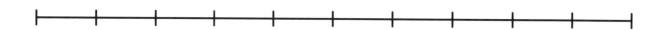

b) $3{\cdot}6 + 0{\cdot}8 = \boxed{}$

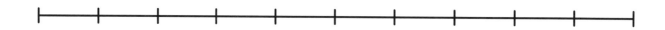

c) $14{\cdot}6 - 0{\cdot}7 = \boxed{}$

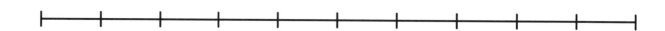

4 Complete the calculations.

a) $0.6 + \boxed{} = 1.3$

b) $1.2 + \boxed{} = 2$

c) $2.5 + \boxed{} = 3.4$

d) $0.18 + \boxed{} = 0.26$

e) $1.1 - \boxed{} = 0.9$

f) $3.5 - \boxed{} = 2.9$

g) $6.7 - \boxed{} = 5.4$

h) $\boxed{} - 0.06 = 0.48$

5 Work out the following calculations in your head.

CHALLENGE

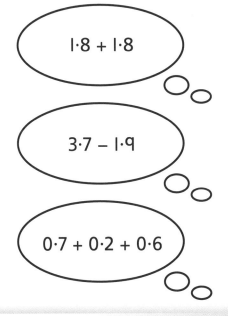

$1.8 + 1.8$

$3.7 - 1.9$

$0.7 + 0.2 + 0.6$

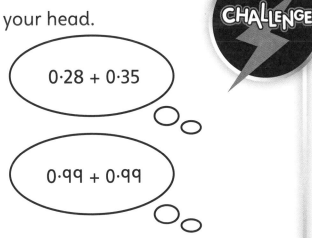

$0.28 + 0.35$

$0.99 + 0.99$

Reflect

Explain to a partner how to find the sum of 1·5 and 0·7 and also the difference between the two numbers.

_____

_____

Date: _____

Add decimals with the same number of decimal places

1 Complete these decimal additions.

a) 0·37 + 0·82

	O	•	Tth	Hth
	0	•	3	7
+	0	•	8	2
		•		

b) 0·82 + 0·78

	O	•	Tth	Hth
	0	•	8	2
+	0	•	7	8
		•		

c) 0·56 + 0·78

	O	•	Tth	Hth
	0	•	5	6
+	0	•	7	8
		•		

d) 0·7 + 0·7

	O	•	Tth
	0	•	7
+	0	•	7
		•	

e) 0·675 + 0·721

	O	•	Tth	Hth	Thth
	0	•	6	7	5
+	0	•	7	2	1
		•			

f) 3·65 + 1·08

	O	•	Tth	Hth
	3	•	6	5
+	1	•	0	8
		•		

2 There are some books for sale in a charity book shop.

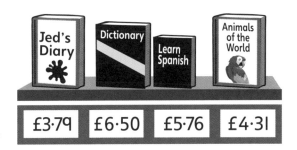

a) How much do the *Dictionary* and *Animals of the World* cost altogether?

£ [ ]

b) Work out the total cost of *Learn Spanish* and *Jed's Diary*.

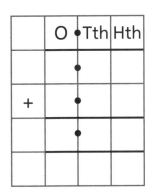

	O	•Tth	Hth
		•	
+		•	
		•	

3 Complete the additions.

a) 2·3 + 4·6

	O	•Tth
	2	• 3
+	4	• 6
		•

b) 3·5 + 5·8

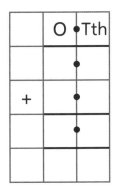

	O	•Tth
		•
+		•
		•

c) 1·98 + 0·77

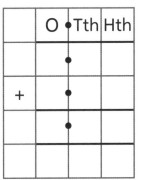

	O	•Tth	Hth
		•	
+		•	
		•	

4 Use the >, < or = signs to complete each number sentence.

a) 0·502 + 4·165 ◯ 3·258 + 0·875

b) 8·62 + 6·18 ◯ 8·63 + 2·71 + 3·26

5 Zac wants to buy the scarf and the magazine.

He adds the amounts.

Discuss with a partner the mistake Zac has made.

£11·20

£3·69

	T	O	•Tth	Hth
		1	• 1	2
+		3	• 6	9
		4	• 8	1
			1	

6 Reena's dad wants to take Reena and her little sister somewhere for her birthday. He has £50. Which activities can they afford to do?

CHALLENGE

	Theatre	Cinema	Zoo	Circus
Adult	£29·50	£15·69	£19·90	£16·60
Child	£9·75	£5·32	£12·50	£8·80

Reflect

Explain how to add 4·53 and 3·78.

Date: _____

Subtract decimals with the same number of decimal places

Textbook 5C p108

1 Work out these calculations.

a) 4·2 – 1·7

	O	•	Tth
	4	•	2
–	1	•	7
		•	

d) 7·26 – 4·83

	O	•	Tth	Hth
	7	•	2	6
–	4	•	8	3
		•		

b) 2·54 – 1·05

	O	•	Tth	Hth
	2	•	5	4
–	1	•	0	5
		•		

e) 2·661 – 0·625

	O	•	Tth	Hth	Thth
	2	•	6	6	1
–	0	•	6	2	5
		•			

c) 8·5 – 3·9

	O	•	Tth
	8	•	5
–	3	•	9
		•	

f) 16·31 – 5·72

	T	O	•	Tth	Hth
	1	6	•	3	1
–		5	•	7	2
			•		

2 Complete the subtractions.

a) 7·56 – 0·49 = ☐

b) 12·52 – 3·92 = ☐

c) 3·005 – 1·486 = ☐

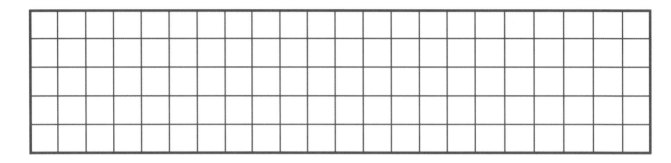

3 Kate has £6·20 in her pocket. She buys a bottle of water for 59p.

Kate does this calculation to work out her change.

What mistake has she made?

_____

_____

_____

	O	•Tth	Hth
	⁵6̸ •¹2		0
–	0 • 5		9
	5 • 7		9

4 Holly is walking 24·5 km for charity. By 3 pm she has walked 18·7 km.

How much farther does Holly have to walk?

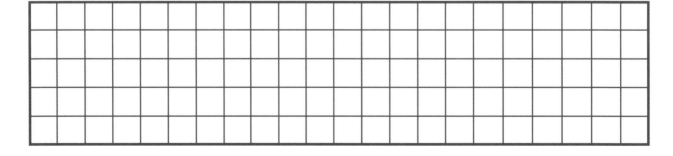

5 Complete the additions.

a) $3 \cdot 21 + \boxed{} = 5 \cdot 49$

b) $12 \cdot 99 = \boxed{} + 5 \cdot 32 + 2 \cdot 69$

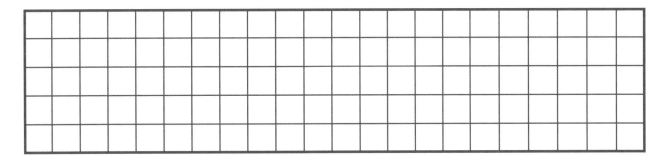

6 How much greater is the difference between A and C than the difference between B and C?

CHALLENGE

The difference between A and C is $\boxed{}$ greater than the difference between B and C.

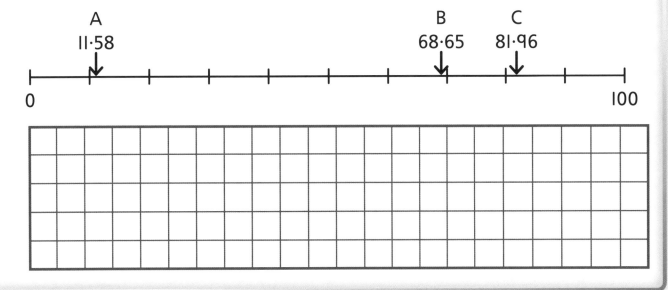

Reflect

What is the same and what is different about these calculations?
Explain to a partner how you would work out the answer to each one.

a) $5 \cdot 8 - 3 \cdot 2$ b) $5 \cdot 8 - 3 \cdot 9$

Date: _____

Add decimals with a different number of decimal places

1 Work out the following calculations.

a) 2·31 + 0·7

	O	•Tth	Hth
	2	3	1
+	0	7	0
		•	

b) 0·514 + 0·65

	O	•Tth	Hth	Thth
	0	5	1	4
+	0	6	5	0
		•		

2 Work out the following calculations.

a) 3·62 + 4·8

	O	•Tth	Hth
	3	6	2
+	4	8	0
		•	

b) 1·96 + 1·258

	O	•Tth	Hth	Thth
	1	9	6	0
+	1	2	5	8
		•		

3 Complete the calculations.

a) 4·7 + 33·64

	T	O	•Tth	Hth
			•	
+			•	
			•	

b) 9·5 + 1·872

	T	O	•Tth	Hth	Thth
			•		
+			•		
			•		

4 **a)** 16·9 + 11·87

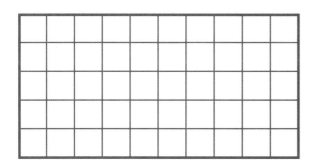

b) 118·7 + 3·952

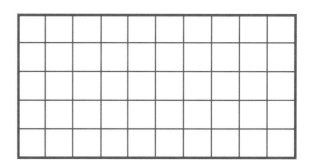

5 Zac is working out 53·49 + 3·7. Explain to a partner the mistake Zac has made. What is the correct answer?

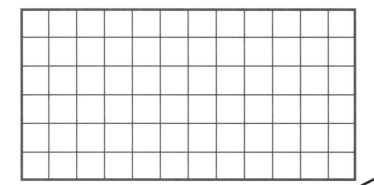

	T	O	•Tth	Hth
	5	3	• 4	9
+		3	•	7
	5	6	• 5	6
			₁	

6 Is Danny's statement true?

Answer always, sometimes or never.

_____

Give some examples to support your answer.

Adding a number with 2 decimal places to a number with 1 decimal place will give an answer with 2 decimal places.

Danny

7 Find the sum of A and B.

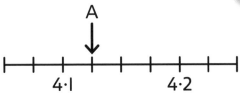

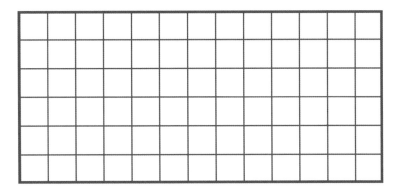

8 Work out these calculations in your head.

a) $3 + 0·45 = \boxed{}$

d) $2 + 9 + 3·4 = \boxed{}$

b) $17 + 8·725 = \boxed{}$

e) $380 \text{ m} + 70·85 \text{ m} = \boxed{}$ m

c) $3·67 \text{ kg} + 7 \text{ kg} = \boxed{}$ kg

f) $28·513 + 48 + 399 = \boxed{}$

Reflect

What are the most important things to remember when adding decimals with a different number of decimal places?

_____

_____

_____

_____

Date: _____

Subtract decimals with a different number of decimal places

1 Complete the column subtractions.

a) 7 – 3·8

	O	•	Tth
	7	•	0
–	3	•	8
		•	

d) 1·765 – 0·3

	O	•	Tth	Hth	Thth
		•			
–		•			
		•			

b) 0·95 – 0·4

	O	•	Tth	Hth
	0	•	9	5
–	0	•	4	0
		•		

e) 0·8 – 0·495

	O	•	Tth	Hth	Thth
		•			
–		•			
		•			

c) 12·8 – 4·35

	T	O	•	Tth	Hth
	1	2	•	8	0
–		4	•	3	5
			•		

f) 5 – 0·176

	O	•	Tth	Hth	Thth
		•			
–		•			
		•			

Textbook 5C p116

2 Bella works out 5 – 2·84 by doing 4·99 – 2·83.

Use Bella's method to answer these calculations.

a) 8 – 2·807= ☐   b) 12 – 4·91 = ☐   c) 16 – 1·8 = ☐

3 a) How much more does the cap cost than the suncream?

£5   £3·92

The cap costs £ ☐ more than the suncream.

b) Mary uses 18·7 ml of suncream.

How much is left?

There is ☐ ml of suncream left.

4 How much more milk than lemonade is there?

There is ☐ l more milk than lemonade.

5 These two cards have a difference of 1·55. What could the sum of the two cards be?

CHALLENGE

How many answers can you find?

| 19·7 | ? |

Reflect

How can you use a number line to show that 7 – 2·4 is the same as 6·9 – 2·3?

Date: _____

Problem solving with decimals

1   Work out the missing values on the bar models.

a)

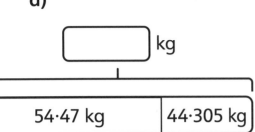

b)

c)

£28·98

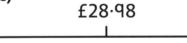

2 Toshi drives 26·3 km to work. He then drives 6·85 km to his gran's house.

How far does he drive in total?

Toshi drives [ ] km in total.

3 What is the mass of the grape?

16·4 g   20·95 g

The mass of the grape is [ ] g.

4 Circle the two numbers that add up to 1·2 and have a difference of 0·78.

| 0·8 | 0·12 | 0·21 | 0·90 | 0·99 | 1·12 |

5 Complete the calculation.

$100 - 1·0 - 0·1 - 0·01 - 0·001 =$ ☐

6 Isla has £20. She spends £3·20 on a magazine. She also buys a book that costs £5·90 more than the magazine.

How much change should Isla receive in total?

Reflect

Look at the bar models in question 1. Write a question that you could solve using one of the bar models.

Date: _____

Problem solving with decimals ❷

1 Amelia buys three items.

How much do the three items cost in total?

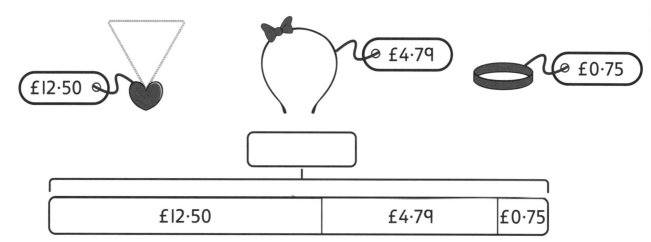

£12·50   £4·79   £0·75

| £12·50 | £4·79 | £0·75 |

The total cost of the three items is £ [   ] .

2 Danny buys two items for his dog. He buys a chew toy costing £4·67 and a lead that costs £2·85 more than the chew toy. He pays with a £20 note.

How much change does Danny get?

93

3 A bucket has 8·75l l of water in it. Amal pours a further 7·5 l into the bucket. 1·27 l of water spill out because the bucket is full.

How much water does the bucket hold?

4 Choose three numbers from the cards that make the calculation true.

$\boxed{} + \boxed{} - \boxed{} = 10$

| 0·345 | 2·233 | 3·578 | 8·655 | 12·178 |

5 The diagram shows three identical rectangular paving slabs. They are put together with their edges touching.

What is the length of the side marked A?

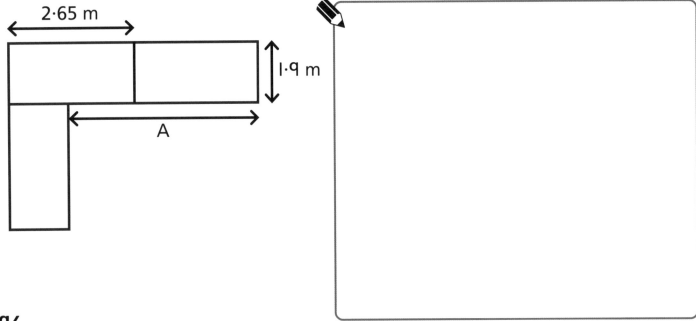

2·65 m

1·9 m

A

6 When added together, these two cards total 9·2.

What is the difference between the cards?

4·59   ?

7 Kate and Richard have both saved some money.

Richard needs to save another £1·20 to make £100.

After paying £24·78 for stationery, Kate has £36·98 less than Richard. How much more money had Richard saved originally than Kate?

CHALLENGE

Reflect

Write a problem-solving question with the answer 3·21 kg. Ask a partner to check the answer.

Date: _____

Decimal sequences

1 Work out the missing numbers in each sequence.

a) 4·6, 4·7, 4·8, ⬚ , ⬚ , ⬚ , ⬚

b) 11·5, 11·9, ⬚ , 12·7, ⬚ , 13·5, ⬚ , ⬚

c) ⬚ , ⬚ , 15·65, 15·6, 15·55, ⬚ , ⬚

2 Complete the numbers on the number line.

a)

0·76   0·77   ⬚ ⬚ ⬚ ⬚ ⬚ ⬚

b)

5·615   5·620   ⬚   5·630   ⬚ ⬚   5·645   ⬚

3 Kate is counting on by the same amount each time.

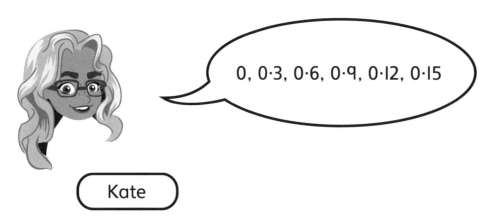

0, 0·3, 0·6, 0·9, 0·12, 0·15

Kate

Explain to a partner the mistake Kate has made.

4 Complete the sequences and write whether each rule is true or false.

a) 10·1, 10·3, 10·5, 10·7, ☐

The rule is 'add 0·2'.

_____

c) 3·0, 2·25, 1·5, 0·75, ☐

The rule is 'subtract 0·25'.

_____

b) 39·57, 39·60, 39·63, 39·66, ☐

The rule is 'add 0·3'.

_____

d) 0·4, 0·52, 0·64, 0·76, ☐

The rule is 'add 0·12'.

_____

5 Max is counting on by 0·02 each time.

He starts at 12·45.

What are the next three numbers Max will say?

☐ , ☐ , ☐

12·45, 12·47 …

Max

6 Complete the sequences.

Tell a partner the rule for each sequence.

a) 0·21, 0·42, 0·63, ☐ , 1·05, 1·26, ☐

b) 11·3, ☐ , 12·1, ☐ , ☐ , 13·3, 13·7

c) 7·68, 7·61, 7·54, 7·47, ☐ , ☐ , 7·26

7 Seven cones are spaced equally apart for a running race.

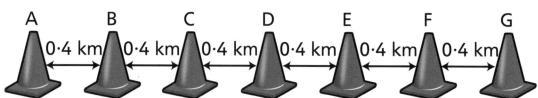

In round I, Toshi starts at A, runs to B and then back to A.

In round 2, he then runs from A to C and back to A.

He continues in the same pattern until round 6, when he runs A to G and back to A.

Complete the table to show how far Toshi runs each round and in total.

Round	I	2	3	4	5	6
Distance travelled in round (km)						
Total distance travelled so far (km)						

Reflect

Make a sequence using decimal numbers. Ask a partner to continue the sequence. What rule did you use?

_____

_____

_____

Date: _____

Multiply by 10

1 Use the place value grids to help you complete these multiplications.

a) $2·4 \times 10 = \boxed{}$

b) $0·13 \times 10 = \boxed{}$

T	O	•	Tth
	① ① ... (10 rows)		0·1 0·1 0·1 0·1 ... (10 rows)

O	•	Tth	Hth
		0·1 ... (10 rows)	0·01 0·01 0·01 ... (10 rows)

2 Complete the multiplications.

a) $1·3 \times 10 = \boxed{}$

H	T	O	•	Tth	Hth	Thth
		1	•	3		

c) $13·5 \times 10 = \boxed{}$

H	T	O	•	Tth	Hth	Thth
	1	3	•	5		

b) $1·35 \times 10 = \boxed{}$

H	T	O	•	Tth	Hth	Thth
		1	•	3	5	

d) $0·135 \times 10 = \boxed{}$

H	T	O	•	Tth	Hth	Thth
		0	•	1	3	5

Textbook 5C p132

3 Olivia says, '14·8 × 10 = 14·80.'

What mistake has Olivia made?

What is the correct answer?

_____

_____

4 Draw lines to match each multiplication to its answer.

| 0·003 × 10 | 3·53 × 10 | 0·03 × 10 | 10 × 0·353 | 0·3 × 10 | 10 × 3·003 | 0·0353 × 10 |

0·03   3   35·3   30·03   0·353   0·3   3·53

5 Complete the multiplications.

a) 5·8 × 10 = ☐

b) 5·82 × 10 = ☐

c) 24·9 × 10 = ☐

d) 1·09 × 10 = ☐

e) 21·08 × 10 = ☐

f) 0·198 × 10 = ☐

g) 10 × 21·08 = ☐

h) 0·019 × 10 = ☐

i) ☐ = 3·09 × 10

j) 0·04 × 10 = ☐

k) ☐ = 3·099 × 10

l) 0·004 × 10 = ☐

m) ☐ = 30·99 × 10

n) 0·040 × 10 = ☐

6 a) Luis is working out the missing number in $\boxed{} \times 10 = 12 \cdot 5$.

He thinks the missing number is 125. Is Luis correct? Explain your answer.

_____

_____

b) Work out the missing numbers.

$\boxed{} \times 10 = 15$ $\boxed{} \times 10 = 9 \cdot 2$ $\boxed{} \times 10 = 1 \cdot 73$

$\boxed{} \times 10 = 25$ $10 \times \boxed{} = 15 \cdot 2$ $\boxed{} \times 10 = 17 \cdot 3$

---

7 Mo's stride is 0·8 metres long. Lexi's stride is 0·65 metres long. **CHALLENGE**
They each take 20 strides.

How much further has Mo travelled than Lexi?

Mo has travelled $\boxed{}$ m further than Lexi.

Reflect

Explain what happens to the digits when you multiply a decimal number by 10.

_____

_____

Date: _____

Multiply by 10, 100 and 1,000

1 Complete the place value grids to work out the answers.

a)

$7.9 \times 10 \quad = \boxed{}$

$7.9 \times 100 \quad = \boxed{}$

$7.9 \times 1{,}000 = \boxed{}$

Th	H	T	O	Tth	Hth
			7	9	

b)

$2.19 \times 10 \quad = \boxed{}$

$2.19 \times 100 \quad = \boxed{}$

$2.19 \times 1{,}000 = \boxed{}$

Th	H	T	O	Tth	Hth
			2	1	9

c) $0.84 \times 100 = \boxed{}$

Th	H	T	O	Tth	Hth
			0	8	4

d) $0.7 \times 1{,}000 = \boxed{}$

Th	H	T	O	Tth	Hth
			0	7	

e) $0.05 \times 100 = \boxed{}$

Th	H	T	O	Tth	Hth

f) $1{,}000 \times 1.7$

Th	H	T	O	Tth	Hth

102

2 Complete the calculations.

a) $0.4 \times 100 = \boxed{}$

$0.04 \times 100 = \boxed{}$

$0.004 \times 100 = \boxed{}$

$100 \times 0.4 = \boxed{}$

b) $1.7 \times 100 = \boxed{}$

$1.7 \times 1,000 = \boxed{}$

$0.17 \times 1,000 = \boxed{}$

c) $\boxed{} \times 100 = 912$

$\boxed{} \times 100 = 91.2$

$\boxed{} \times 1,000 = 9.12$

$1,000 \times \boxed{} = 91.2$

d) $4.5 \times \boxed{} = 450$

$0.045 \times \boxed{} = 4.5$

$0.045 \times \boxed{} = 0.45$

$0.045 \times \boxed{} = 45$

3 a) Sofia buys 1,000 cans of orange juice for the school café. One can contains 0·335 litres of juice.

How many litres of orange juice did Sofia buy?

b) The length of a blue straw is 0·11 m. The length of a red straw is 0·09 m.

What is the total length of 100 blue and 100 red straws?

4. Complete the missing numbers in this multiplication grid.

Number			0·38		0·012
×		3	380	76	
×	12·7				1·2

5. Use the number cards to find three ways to complete each calculation.

CHALLENGE

| 10 | 100 | 1,000 | 6·8 | 0·68 | 0·068 |

a) ⬚ × ⬚ = 68

⬚ × ⬚ = 68

⬚ × ⬚ = 68

b) ⬚ × ⬚ = ⬚ × ⬚

⬚ × ⬚ = ⬚ × ⬚

⬚ × ⬚ = ⬚ × ⬚

Reflect

Complete the sentences:

- Multiplying by 100 is the same as multiplying by ⬚ and ⬚ again.

- Multiplying by 1,000 is the same as multiplying by ⬚ and ⬚ and ⬚ again.

Show a partner how you can use a place value grid to multiply by 100 or 1,000.

Divide by 10

1 Use the place value grids to help you work out the division.

$1.2 \div 10 =$ ⬚

T	O	•	Tth	Hth
	1	•	2	
		•		

O	•	Tth	Hth

2 Work out these divisions.

a) $4.5 \div 10 =$ ⬚

Th	H	T	O	•	Tth	Hth
			4	•	5	
				•		

c) $45 \div 10 =$ ⬚

Th	H	T	O	•	Tth	Hth
		4	5	•		
				•		

b) $0.45 \div 10 =$ ⬚

H	T	O	•	Tth	Hth	Thth
			•			
			•			

d) $4.52 \div 10 =$ ⬚

H	T	O	•	Tth	Hth	Thth
			•			
			•			

3 What number should go in each part of the bar? Complete the calculation.

23

$$\boxed{} \div \boxed{} = \boxed{}$$

4 10 apples have a total mass of 2·8 kg. Each of the apples has the same mass.

What is the mass of one apple?

The mass of one apple is $\boxed{}$ kg.

5 Work out the following missing numbers.

a) $603 \div 10 = \boxed{}$

d) $75{\cdot}3 \div \boxed{} = 7{\cdot}53$

g) $0{\cdot}035 = \boxed{} \div 10$

b) $160{\cdot}3 \div 10 = \boxed{}$

e) $\boxed{} \div 10 = 0{\cdot}08$

h) $8{\cdot}719 = \boxed{} \div 10$

c) $16{\cdot}31 \div 10 = \boxed{}$

f) $3{\cdot}978 \div 10 = \boxed{}$

i) $3{\cdot}895 \times 10 = \boxed{} \div 10$

6 Is Max correct? Explain any mistakes.

_____

_____

_____

_____

10 books costs £35, so each book costs £3·5.

Max

7 **a)** What is the cost of 100 ml of lemonade?

100 ml of lemonade costs £ ⬚ .

b) What is the cost of 200 g of cocoa?
Explain your answer.

200 g of cocoa costs £ ⬚ .

Cocoa £12 1 kg

Lemonade £1·80 1 l

_____

_____

CHALLENGE

8 Toshi has 2·5 kg of hot chocolate powder. He makes 10 cups of hot chocolate every week for 10 weeks before it runs out.

How much powder does he use in each cup? Give your answer in kg.

Toshi uses ⬚ kg of hot chocolate powder in each cup.

Reflect

Explain how to divide a decimal number by 10.

- _____
- _____

Date: _____

Divide by 10, 100 and 1,000

1 Use the place value grids to answer these questions.

a) 23 ÷ 100 = ☐

H	T	O	• Tth	Hth	Thth
	2	3 •			

c) 5·2 ÷ 100 = ☐

H	T	O	• Tth	Hth	Thth
		5 •	2		
			•		

b) 145 ÷ 1,000 = ☐

H	T	O	• Tth	Hth	Thth
		•			
		•			

d) 13 ÷ 1,000 = ☐

H	T	O	• Tth	Hth	Thth
		•			
		•			

2 Use the tenths grid to show if Bella is correct.

Explain your answer.

Dividing by 10 and then 10 again is the same as dividing by 100.

Bella

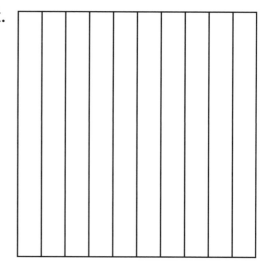

_____

_____

_____

_____

3 Write true or false under each calculation. Correct those that are incorrect.

a) $9 \div 100 = 0.09$

c) $53 \div 100 = 0.053$

e) $8.7 \div 100 = 0.87$

_____

_____

_____

b) $7 \div 1,000 = 0.007$

d) $75 \div 1,000 = 0.075$

f) $9.1 \div 1,000 = 0.00091$

_____

_____

_____

4 Draw lines to match the calculations that give the same answer. Not all have a pair.

| $0.8 \div 100$ | $0.18 \div 100$ | $10.8 \div 100$ | $0.108 \div 10$ |

| $108 \div 1,000$ | $0.08 \div 100$ | $8 \div 1,000$ | $1.8 \div 1,000$ | $1.08 \div 100$ |

5 Complete the calculations.

a) $37 \div \boxed{} = 3.7$

$37 \div \boxed{} = 0.37$

$37 \div \boxed{} = 0.037$

b) $\boxed{} \div 10 = 0.12$

$\boxed{} \div 100 = 0.12$

$\boxed{} \div 1,000 = 0.12$

6 Each day Zac and Jamie put some money in their money boxes.

After 100 days Zac has £18 and Jamie has £124.

If they always put in the same amount each day, how much more money did Jamie save each day in pounds?
Give the answer as a decimal.

Jamie saved £ ☐ more each day.

7 Each shape represents a different number. Find the missing values.

CHALLENGE

$\blacksquare \div 10 = \blacktriangle \times 100 = 0.098$ $\bigstar \times 10 = 0.61 \div 100 = \bullet$

$\blacksquare =$ ☐ $\bigstar =$ ☐

$\blacktriangle =$ ☐ $\bullet =$ ☐

Reflect

Reena thinks that $0.351 \div 10 = 3.51 \div 100$ and $3.51 \div 100 = 35.1 \div 1{,}000$.
Is Reena correct? Explain your answer.

End of unit check

My journal

1   Ebo is working out 12 − 4·35.

    a) Show two different ways Ebo could do this.

    What advice would you give Ebo?

    _____

    _____

    b) What mistakes should Ebo be careful not to make when subtracting decimals?

    _____

    _____

2 What is the same and what is different about these calculations?

25 + 2·95   12·47 + 13·48   18·3 + 9·65

Power check

How do you feel about your work in this unit?

Power puzzle

The aim is to find a path from 2 to 0·002. You can move right, left, up or down. At each step, you must do the calculation in the box.

2	÷ 100	÷ 10	× 100	× 10	÷ 100
÷ 1,000	× 100	× 10	÷ 10	× 100	× 10
× 10	÷ 100	× 10	÷ 10	× 100	÷ 1,000
× 100	÷ 10	× 1,000	× 100	× 10	0·002

How many different paths can you find? Use the place value grid to help you.

TTh	Th	H	T	O	•	Tth	Hth	Thth

Now find a route where the answer is 2.

2	÷ 100	÷ 10	× 100	× 10	÷ 100
÷ 1,000	× 100	× 10	÷ 10	× 100	× 10
× 10	÷ 100	× 10	÷ 10	× 100	÷ 1,000
× 100	÷ 10	× 1,000	× 100	× 10	2

Date: _____

Understand negative numbers

1 **a)** A submarine is on the surface of the sea.

It goes down 3 metres.

What level is it at now?

☐ metres

b) Draw the new position of the submarine.

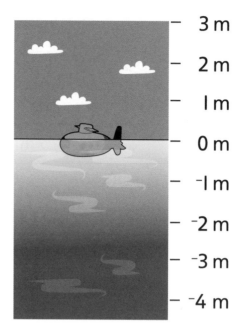

2 What is the temperature shown on each thermometer?

a)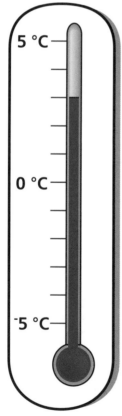

b)

c)

d)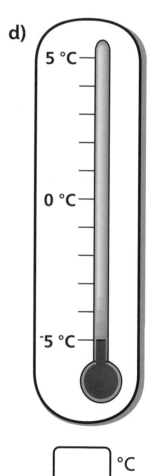

☐ °C   ☐ °C   ☐ °C   ☐ °C

3 Write in the missing numbers.

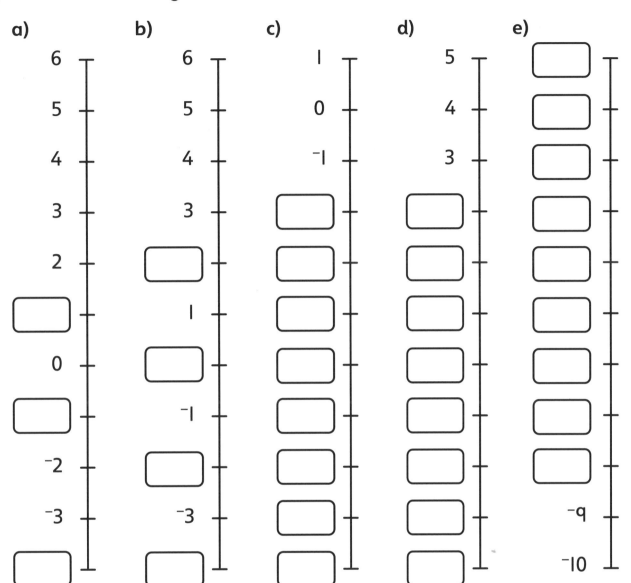

a)   b)   c)   d)   e)

4 Write the missing numbers in each sequence.

a) 3, 2, 1, 0, ☐ , ☐ , ☐

b) ⁻5, ⁻4, ⁻3, ⁻2, ⁻1, ☐ , ☐ , ☐

c) 6, ☐ , 4, ☐ , 2, ☐ , 0, ☐ , ☐ , ☐

d) ☐ , ☐ , ⁻4, ⁻3, ☐ , ☐ , ☐ , ☐ , ☐

CHALLENGE

5 Complete each label.

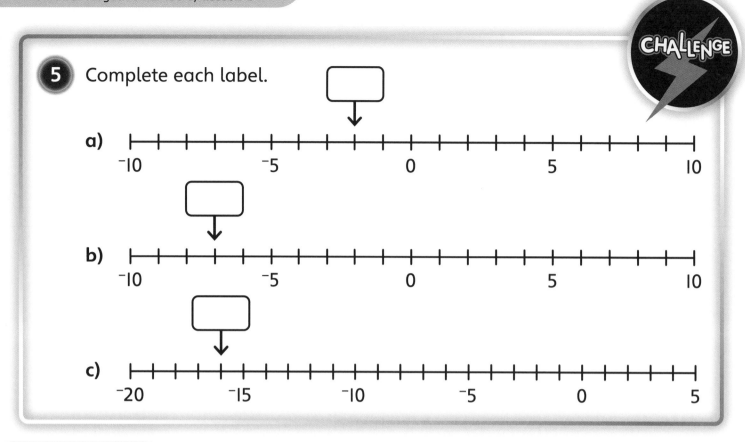

a)
```
-10          -5          0          5          10
```

b)
```
-10          -5          0          5          10
```

c)
```
-20       -15       -10       -5        0        5
```

Reflect

A board game looks like this:

| -8 | -7 | -6 | -5 | -4 | -3 | -2 | -1 | 0 | 1 | 2 | 3 | 4 | 5 | 6 | 7 | 8 |

Roll a dice. You can choose to jump either left or right. Count the numbers as you land on them.

Your aim is to land on exactly -8. If you fall off the end, you lose the game!

Try playing with a partner.

I like this game. I'm going to draw my own board from -20 to 20.

I will play a few games, then think of some new rules to try.

Date: _____

Count through zero

1 Complete the thermometers and write the temperatures.

a)

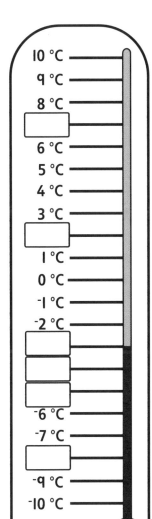

b)

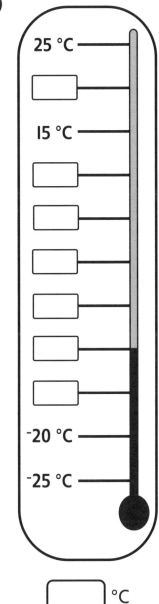

c)

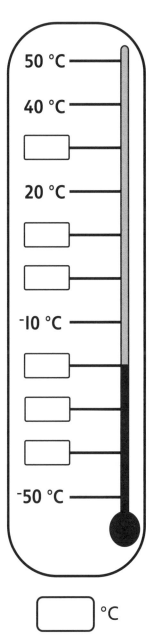

a) [ ] °C   b) [ ] °C   c) [ ] °C

2 Complete the missing numbers.

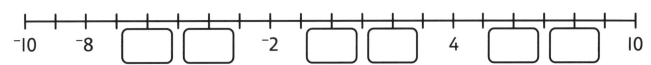

↓ Textbook 5C p156

3 Write the numbers shown by the arrows.

a)
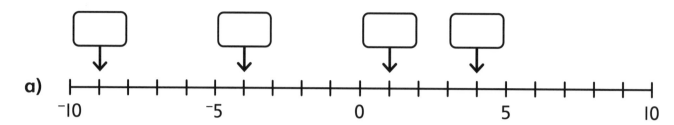

b)
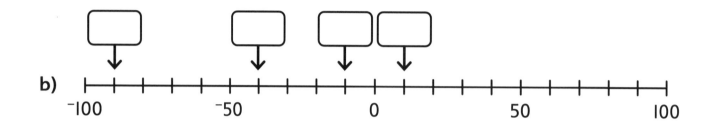

c)
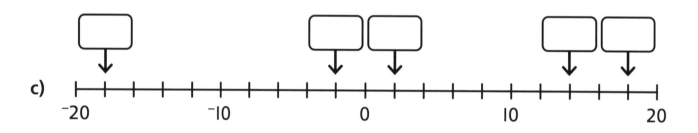

4 Join each number to the number line.

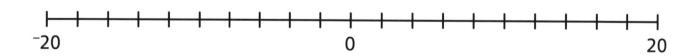

5 Complete the counting sequence.

a)

11	9	7	5	3	1	⁻1	⁻3	⁻5	⁻7

b)

⁻11	⁻9	⁻7	⁻5	⁻3	⁻1	1	3	5	7

c)

⁻81	⁻71	⁻61	⁻51	⁻41	⁻31	⁻21	⁻11	⁻1	9

d)

⁻20	⁻15	⁻10	⁻5	0	5	10	15	20	25

e)

⁻21	⁻16	⁻11	⁻6	⁻1	4	9	14	19	24

Reflect

Play a game as a class.

Sit or stand in a circle. Choose someone to start at ⁻100.

Count on in different sized steps.

Try counting back from 100. Can you predict who will be first to pass 0?

Date: _____

Compare and order negative numbers

1 Complete the comparisons using <, > or =.

a) 0 ◯ ⁻5

c) 0 ◯ ⁻1

e) ⁻1 ◯ 0

b) ⁻5 ◯ 6

d) ⁻8 ◯ 5

f) 8 ◯ ⁻8

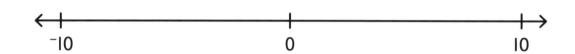

2 Complete the comparisons.

a) ⁻20 ◯ ⁻5

c) ⁻6 ◯ ⁻7

e) ⁻1 ◯ ⁻2

b) ⁻100 ◯ ⁻60

d) ⁻85 ◯ ⁻84

f) ⁻1 ◯ ⁻999

3 Order this set of numbers from smallest to greatest.

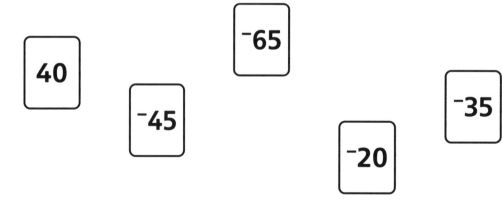

smallest ▢ < ▢ < ▢ < ▢ < ▢ greatest

4 Estimate the numbers shown by the arrows.

a)

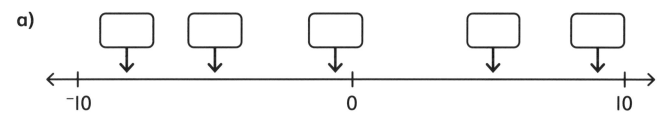

b)

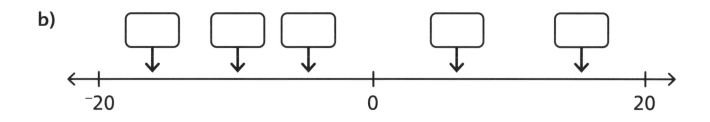

c)

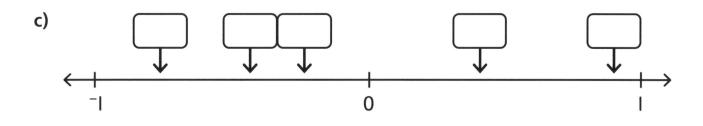

d)

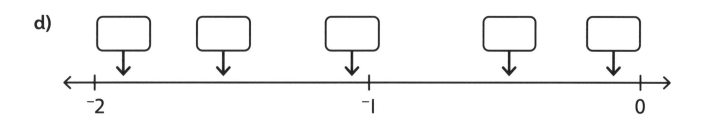

5 Explain the mistakes on each of these number lines.

a)
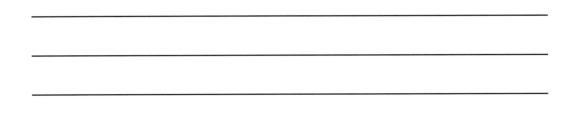

_____

_____

_____

_____

b)
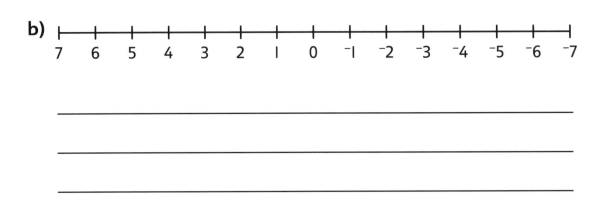

_____

_____

_____

_____

Reflect

Max says, '⁻1 is less than ⁻4 because 1 is smaller than 4.'

Do you agree with Max? Explain your answer.

_____

_____

Find the difference

1 The thermometers show the temperatures in two cities.

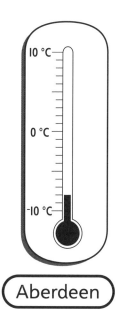

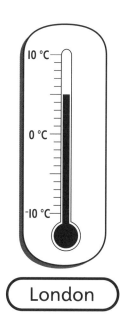

Aberdeen   London

a) What is the temperature in Aberdeen? ☐ °C

b) What is the temperature in London? ☐ °C

c) How many degrees warmer is it in London than in Aberdeen? ☐ °C

2 The two thermometers show the temperatures inside Max's fridge and freezer.

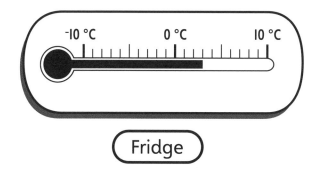

Fridge

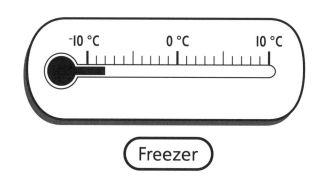

Freezer

How much colder is the temperature in the freezer than in the fridge?

☐ °C colder.

Textbook 5C p164

3 The table shows the temperatures in four cities around the world.

Calgary	Dubai	Moscow	Istanbul
⁻13 °C	19 °C	⁻5 °C	4 °C

a) Mark the temperature in each city on the number line.

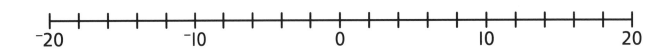

⁻20   ⁻10   0   10   20

b) How many degrees warmer is Istanbul than Calgary? ⬚ °C

c) Put the temperatures in order, starting with the coldest.

coldest   ⬚ °C, ⬚ °C, ⬚ °C, ⬚ °C   warmest

d) During the night, the temperature in Istanbul falls by 8 °C.

What is the temperature in the city during the night? ⬚ °C

4 Toshi goes from floor 12 to floor ⁻3.

a) How many floors does Toshi travel down?

Toshi travels down ⬚ floors.

b) Holly travels up 8 floors from floor ⁻1.

Which floor is Holly now on?

Holly is now on floor ⬚.

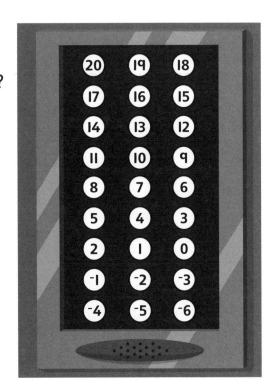

5 The base of a mountain lies 300 m below sea level.

The top of the mountain is 2,000 m above sea level.

How tall is the mountain from base to top?

The mountain is ⬚ m tall.

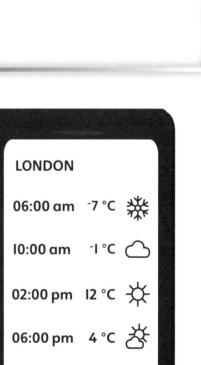

6 The top of an iceberg is 12 m above sea level.

The depth of the iceberg below sea level is 8 times the height of the iceberg above sea level.

How tall is the iceberg in total?

The iceberg is ⬚ m tall in total.

CHALLENGE

Reflect

Write two sentences that describe the changes in temperature through the day. For example, between 6 am and 10 am the temperature increased by 6 °C.

LONDON

06:00 am	-7 °C	❄
10:00 am	-1 °C	☁
02:00 pm	12 °C	☀
06:00 pm	4 °C	🌤
10:00 pm	-2 °C	❄

_____

_____

_____

_____

_____

Date: _____

End of unit check

My journal

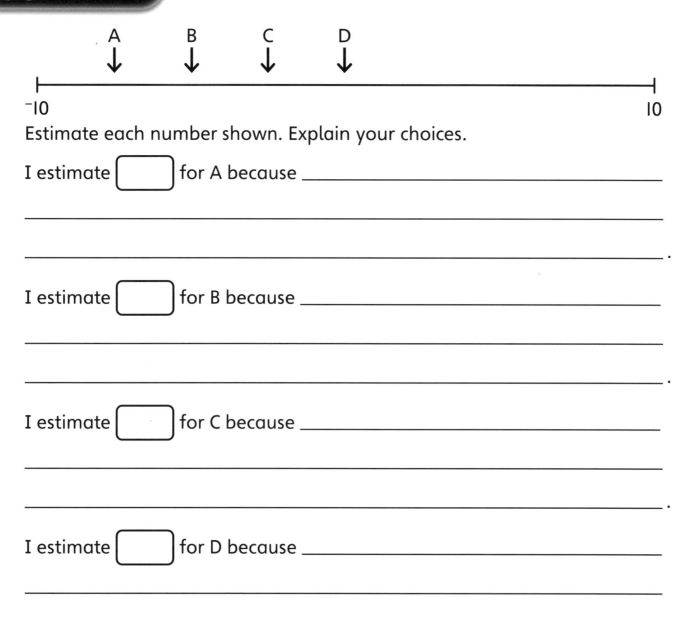

Estimate each number shown. Explain your choices.

I estimate [ ] for A because _____

_____

_____ .

I estimate [ ] for B because _____

_____

_____ .

I estimate [ ] for C because _____

_____

_____ .

I estimate [ ] for D because _____

_____

_____ .

→ Textbook 5C p168

Power check

How do you feel about your work in this unit?

Power puzzle

Zac makes two number sequences using some number cards.

The sequences have different amounts of terms in them.

One sequence goes up by the same amount each time.

One sequence goes down by the same amount each time.

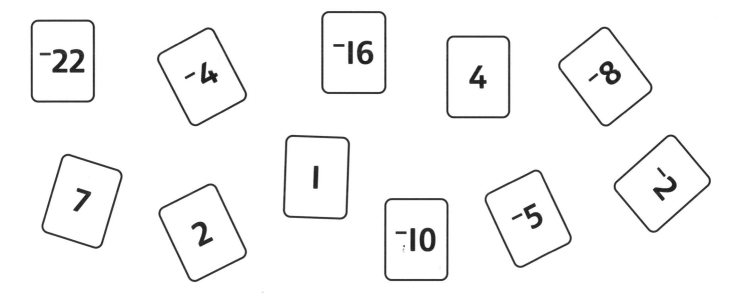

He mixes the sequences up.

Work out the two sequences.

Now make two of your own sequences using negative and positive numbers.

Mix up the numbers in your sequences.
See if a partner can work out your sequences.

Date: _____

Kilograms and kilometres

1 Complete the conversions.

a) 5 km = [ ] m

   8 km = [ ] m

   14 km = [ ] m

   54 km = [ ] m

   103 km = [ ] m

c) 3·2 km = [ ] m

   5·9 km = [ ] m

   12·5 km = [ ] m

   0·8 km = [ ] m

   1·75 km = [ ] m

b) 5,000 m = [ ] km

   9,000 m = [ ] km

   18,000 m = [ ] km

   70,000 m = [ ] km

   140,000 m = [ ] km

d) 1,900 m = [ ] km

   3,800 m = [ ] km

   14,500 m = [ ] km

   1,050 m = [ ] km

   340 m = [ ] km

2 Complete the table.

From	To	Distance in m	Distance in km
Swansea	Mumbles	[ ]	7·9 km
London	Birmingham	162,000 m	[ ]
Glasgow	Edinburgh	67,100 m	[ ]
Manchester	Liverpool	[ ]	50 km
Lynton	Lynmouth	1,300 m	[ ]

128

3 Which method would you use for these conversions? Write the letters in the correct circle.

A Convert the length of your school hall (in metres) into kilometres.

÷ 1,000   × 1,000

B Calculate the mass of a bag of potatoes (in kilograms) in grams.

C Work out what a motorway sign showing kilometres would show as metres.

D Change the mass of a chocolate bar (in grams) into kilograms.

4 Complete the conversions.

a) 12 kg = [   ] g

b) 8,000 g = [   ] kg

c) 6,500 g = [   ] kg

d) 3·4 kg = [   ] g

e) 10 kg 200 g = [   ] g

10 kg 200 g = [   ] kg

f) 4 kg 3,000 g = [   ] g

4 kg 3,000 g = [   ] kg

5 Explain the mistake Kate has made and how to find the correct answer.

My dog has a mass of 27·5 kg. There are 1,000 g in a kilogram, so to convert this into grams, I need to divide 27·5 by 1,000.

Kate

_____

_____

_____

6　A lorry has this dial to show the distance it has travelled.

It drives to deliver a parcel and the dial
shows a 4, a 5 and a 0.
It does not show a whole number of kilometres.

How many metres could the
lorry have travelled?

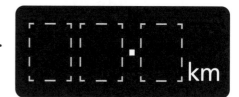

7　Ambika has five bags of pebbles. Their masses are 18,000 g,
700 g, 5,500 g, 8,000 g and 230 g.

How many of the bags weigh a whole number of kilograms?
Explain your answer.

Reflect

Explain how to convert 12,500 g into kilograms.

Millimetres and millilitres

Textbook 5C p176

1 Complete the conversions.

a) 2,000 ml = ☐ l

b) 7,000 ml = ☐ l

c) 23,000 ml = ☐ l

d) 3 litres = ☐ ml

e) 3·5 litres = ☐ ml

f) 8,200 ml = ☐ l

g) 16,900 ml = ☐ l

h) 1·75 l = ☐ ml

i) 0·3 l = ☐ ml

j) 0·03 l = ☐ ml

2 Complete the conversions.

a) 1,000 mm = ☐ m

b) 2,000 mm = ☐ m

c) 9 m = ☐ mm

d) 3,500 mm = ☐ m

e) 6·7 m = ☐ mm

f) 12,000 mm = ☐ m

g) 6·75 m = ☐ mm

3 a) A sunflower is 3,000 mm tall.

How many metres tall is it? ☐ m

b) A bottle of lemonade holds 1·25 l.

How many millilitres does it hold? ☐ ml

4 **a)** Draw an arrow to show 0·7 l on the jug.

b) Draw an arrow to show 0·35 l on the jug.

```
— 1,000 ml
— 900
— 800
— 700
— 600
— 500
— 400
— 300
— 200
— 100
— 0
```

5 Complete the conversions.

a) 4,000 ml = [   ] l

b) 15 l = [   ] ml

c) 7·2 l = [   ] l and [   ] ml

d) 1,600 ml = [   ] l

e) 12 l 500 ml = [   ] ml

12 l 500 ml = [   ] l

f) 9 l 2,500 ml = [   ] ml

9 l 2,500 ml = [   ] l

6 Lee measures the length of his table in metres and converts it into centimetres. Mo measures the same distance in millimetres.

Explain to a partner how you know Mo is correct.

My number is 10 times Lee's!

Mo

7 The three cups below hold different amounts of liquid.

Amelia uses the cups to measure these amounts of water: 0·5 l, 0·25 l, 0·35 l and 0·375 l.

To do this, she may have to fill a cup more than once. But she only uses three cupfuls each time. Complete the table to show which cups she uses each time.

First cup	Second cup	Third cup	Total
			0·5 l
			0·25 l
			0·35 l
			0·375 l

Reflect

Is Danny right or wrong? Explain your answer.

To convert 5·6 cm into millimetres, I need to divide by 10 because 10 mm equals 1 cm.

Danny

_____

_____

_____

Date: _____

Convert units of length

1 Complete the bar models to help show each conversion.

1 cm
☐ mm

1 m
☐ cm

1 km
☐ m

2 Complete the conversions.

a) 3 cm = ☐ mm

b) 7 cm = ☐ mm

c) 12 cm = ☐ mm

d) 4·3 cm = ☐ mm

e) 0·8 cm = ☐ mm

f) 15·7 cm = ☐ mm

g) 90 mm = ☐ cm

h) 170 mm = ☐ cm

i) 59 mm = ☐ cm

j) 103 mm = ☐ cm

3 Complete the conversions.

a) 200 cm = ☐ m

b) 900 cm = ☐ m

c) 780 cm = ☐ m

d) 90 cm = ☐ m

e) 8 m = ☐ cm

f) 8·3 m = ☐ cm

g) 0·45 m = ☐ cm

4 The tail of a mouse is 142 mm long. How many centimetres is this?

Draw the mouse's tail so that your drawing is the correct length.

5 Year 5 are having a sunflower growing competition. Here are their results:

Name	Lexi	Ebo	Max	Reena
Height of sunflower	1·3 m	$1\frac{1}{4}$ m	123 cm	1,252 mm

Write the children's names in order, put the one with the tallest sunflower first and the one with the shortest sunflower last.

_____   _____   _____   _____

6 The length of a piece of ribbon is 2 m. It has a width of 3 cm.

3 cm ▬▬▬▬▬▬▬▬▬▬▬▬▬▬▬▬▬▬▬▬▬▬▬▬▬▬▬▬▬▬▬▬

2 m

a) Danny says the perimeter of the ribbon is 10 cm. What mistake has he made?

_____

_____

b) Work out the correct perimeter.

The perimeter is ☐ cm = ☐ m.

7 **a)** The length of the smallest dog in the world is 15·2 cm.
Mark its length on this ruler.

CHALLENGE

| 0 10 20 30 40 50 60 70 80 90 100 110 120 130 140 150 160 170 180 190 200 |

mm

b) The longest straw ever used to drink cola in the world is
75·82 m! How many centimetres will the cola need to travel
before you can taste it?

The cola will travel ☐ cm.

c) The narrowest street in the world is 310 mm wide. Would you be
able to walk down it? Explain your answer.

_____

_____

Reflect

Complete the sentences in as many ways as you can.

There are 10 _____ in ☐ _____ .

There are 100 _____ in ☐ _____ .

There are 1,000 _____ in ☐ _____ .

136

Imperial units of length

1 **a)** Draw a circle around each imperial unit.

10-inch pizza

25 m

20 cm wide

6 feet 2 inches

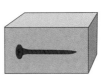

15 mm screws

b) Complete each sentence with one of the cards.

1 inch is approximately _____ .

1 foot is equal to _____ .

1 yard is equal to _____ .

3 feet

$2\frac{1}{2}$ cm

12 inches

2 Use your answers from question 1 b) to help you answer this question.

This snake is 4 feet long.

How many inches long is the snake?

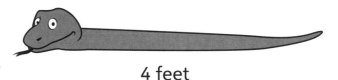

4 feet

☐ × ☐ = ☐

The snake is ☐ inches long.

1 foot			
12 inches			

3 The ruler below shows inches and centimetres but it is incomplete.

Add the missing labels.

												cm
0	2·5	5	7·5									
0	1	2										inches

4 Circle the correct measurement.

a) Which is taller: a 48 inch chimpanzee or a $3\frac{1}{2}$ foot baboon? Show your working.

b) Which is longer: a 6 yard pond or a 21 foot patio? Show your working.

5 The width of this television screen is 55 inches. Complete the bar model and the conversions.

55 inches

55 inches

| 12 inches | 12 inches | 12 inches | 12 inches | 7 in |
| 1 foot | | | | |

= ☐ ft ☐ in

= ☐ yd ☐ ft ☐ in

6 The sat nav in Mr Lopez's car is set to imperial measurements.

It says, 'Turn left in 20 yards. Continue for 100 yards.'

Convert these distances into metres. Show your working.

CHALLENGE

I yard is about the same as 90 cm.

20 yards is about [ ] m. 100 yards is about [ ] m.

Reflect

Jamie says that a typical adult is about 2 feet tall.
What mistake might she have made?

Date: _____

Imperial units of mass

1 Complete the number line. Use it to work out each conversion.

> I pound (1 lb) is the same as 16 ounces (16 oz).

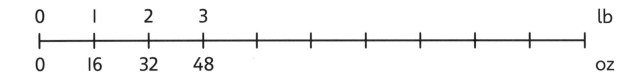

a) 3 lb = ☐ oz

b) ☐ lb = 112 oz

c) 5 lb = ☐ oz

d) 8 lb 2 oz = ☐ oz

e) ☐ lb ☐ oz = 51 oz

f) $\frac{1}{2}$ lb = ☐ oz

g) $\frac{1}{4}$ lb = ☐ oz

h) 4·5 lb = ☐ oz

2 a) What is the mass of the box of oranges in pounds?

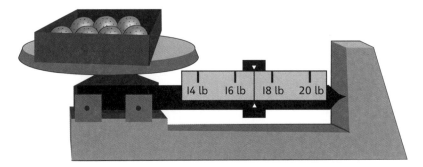

The box of oranges has a mass of ☐ lb.

b) How many ounces is this equal to?

☐ lb = ☐ oz

3 I kg is about the same as 2·2 lb.

Max says that his cat has a mass of about 5 kg.

Complete the bar model to show whether Max is correct.

11 lb

5 kg

I kg				
2·2 lb				

[ ] lb

I lb is about 450 g. I wonder how you can find $3\frac{1}{2}$ lbs in kilograms?

Richard

4 Help Richard solve the problem. Explain your answer.

_____

_____

5 Crack the code!

a) Shade the three measurements that are approximately equal to 10 lb.

	S = 4·5 g	O = 4·5 kg	R = 1·6 oz
	I = 450 g	A = 450 kg	N = 160 oz
	T = 4,500 g	E = 4,500 kg	P = 16 oz

b) Rearrange the three letters you shaded to spell a different imperial unit (equal to 2,240 lb).

The imperial unit is _____ .

141

6 A giant octopus has a mass of about 7 stone and 2 lb.

CHALLENGE

a) What is its mass in pounds?

The giant octopus has a mass of ▢ lb.

1 stone (st) = 14 lb

1 kg = 2·2 lb

b) What is its mass in kilograms?

The giant octopus has a mass of ▢ kg.

Reflect

A small dog has a mass of 14 lb. Describe how you could convert (change) this mass in to metric units.

Date: _____

Imperial units of capacity

1 I pint is approximately equal to 570 ml.

Add 570 each time and complete the bar model.

1 pint	2 pints	3 pints					
570 ml	1,140 ml	1,710 ml					

2 Use the bar model in question 1 to complete these measurements.

a) 5 pints = [ ] ml

b) [ ] pints = 4,560 ml

c) 3 pints = [ ] ml

d) 1 litre 140 ml = [ ] pints

e) [ ] litres [ ] ml = 6 pints

f) [ ] pints = 3·99 litres

g) $\frac{1}{2}$ pint = [ ] millilitres

3 There are 8 pints in a gallon.

Circle the measurement that is nearest to 1 gallon.

4 litres   4 $\frac{1}{2}$ litres   5 litres

Explain your answer.

_____

_____

4 How much milk is in this jug? Give your answer in pints and litres.

The jug contains ☐ pints

= ☐ l

1 pint = approximately 570 ml

5 Three bottles of lemonade contain 200 ml each. Lexi pours them into a jug.

Mark a line on the jug where you think the top of the lemonade will roughly be.

6 Which pond contains the most water?

Complete the number line, then mark each pond on the number line with an arrow.

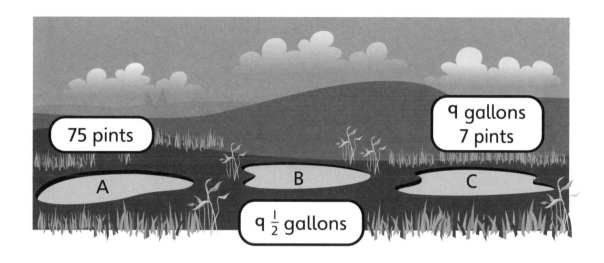

75 pints

9 gallons
7 pints

A B C

$9 \frac{1}{2}$ gallons

```
0      1      2      3                                    gallons
├──────┼──────┼──────┼──────┼──────┼──────┼──────┼──────┼──────┼──────┤
0      8                                                 pints
```

Pond _____ contains the most water.

Reflect

You have been asked to go and buy 2 pints of milk. It is only sold in litres. How many litres would you buy? Explain your answer.

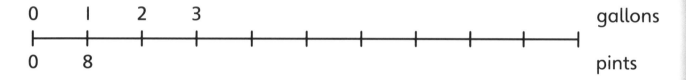

Date: _____

Convert units of time

1 a) How many hours and minutes is a 310 minute rail journey?

b) How many minutes and seconds is a 195 second pop song?

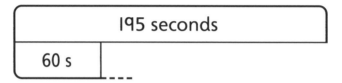

195 seconds

60 s

2 The films below have different running times. Which film is longer?

Draw a bar model to help you find the answer.

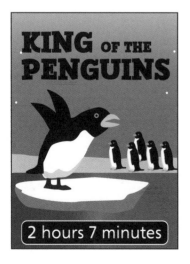

KING OF THE PENGUINS

2 hours 7 minutes

Escape from PLANET Zarg

137 minutes

_____ is longer.

3 Is Ambika correct?
Explain your answer.

4·25 hours is 4 hours and 25 minutes.

Ambika

_____

_____

4 Here are the lengths of the summer holidays for four children.

Name	Kate	Lee	Bella	Mo
Length of holidays	21 July to 2 September	40 days	5 weeks and 4 days	The whole of August plus 10 days

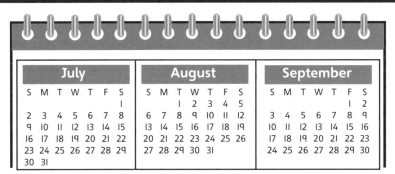

July							August							September						
S	M	T	W	T	F	S	S	M	T	W	T	F	S	S	M	T	W	T	F	S
						1		1	2	3	4	5							1	2
2	3	4	5	6	7	8	6	7	8	9	10	11	12	3	4	5	6	7	8	9
9	10	11	12	13	14	15	13	14	15	16	17	18	19	10	11	12	13	14	15	16
16	17	18	19	20	21	22	20	21	22	23	24	25	26	17	18	19	20	21	22	23
23	24	25	26	27	28	29	27	28	29	30	31			24	25	26	27	28	29	30
30	31																			

Put the children's names in order, from shortest holiday to longest holiday. Show your working.

_____ _____ _____ _____

147

5 These function machines convert from one unit of time into another.

CHALLENGE

This machine converts hours to minutes.

hours → × 60 → minutes

a) Complete these function machines to show what they do.

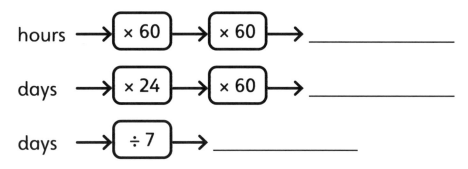

hours → × 60 → × 60 → _____

days → × 24 → × 60 → _____

days → ÷ 7 → _____

b) Draw a function machine to show how you would find the number of minutes in a leap year.

Reflect

Describe how you would convert 30 months into years and months.

_____

_____

_____

Timetables – calculating

1 Look carefully at this coach timetable.

Stop	Coach A	Coach B	Coach C	Coach D	Coach E	Coach F
Birmingham Bus Station	05:45	07:30	09:20	11:15	12:50	14:35
Gilbertstone	06:05	07:50	09:40	11:35	13:10	14:55
Birmingham Airport	06:15	08:00	09:50	11:45	13:20	15:05
Coventry Bus Station	06:40	08:25	10:15	12:10	13:45	15:30
Northampton Bus Station	07:40	09:25	11:15	13:10	14:45	16:30
Luton Airport	08:45	10:30	12:20	14:15	15:50	17:35
Hertford North Station	09:30	11:15	13:05	15:00	16:35	18:20
Stansted Airport	10:20	12:05	13:55	15:50	17:25	19:10

a) Complete the sentences.

There are ☐ rows in the timetable. Each row shows a different

_____ .

There are ☐ columns. Each column shows a different _____ .

The times in the timetable are ☐ hour times.

b) What time does the coach that leaves
Gilbertstone at five minutes past 6 arrive at
Luton Airport?   It arrives at ☐ : ☐ .

c) What time does the ten minutes to 4 arrival at
Luton Airport leave Birmingham Bus Station?   It left at ☐ : ☐ .

d) Complete the sentences.

At ☐ : ☐ Coach D arrives at Luton Airport.

Its next stop is _____ .

It takes ☐ minutes to get there and it arrives at ☐ : ☐ .

2 This is part of a railway timetable.

Grantham	06:31	07:23	08:16	09:32	11:27	12:25
Rauceby	–	07:46	08:40	–	–	–
Sleaford	06:57	07:51	08:45	09:58	11:53	12:50
Boston	07:25	08:18	09:12	10:26	12:19	13:15
Thorpe Culvert	07:47	–	–	10:48	–	–
Wainfleet	07:51	08:43	09:36	10:52	12:44	13:40
Havenhouse	07:55	–	–	10:56	–	–
Skegness	08:05	08:56	09:49	11:06	12:58	13:54

a) Olivia arrives at Boston at 10 o'clock and catches the next train to Skegness. How long is she on the train for?

b) It is 09:33. Mo is at Grantham and has just missed the train! How long will he have to wait for the next train to Skegness?

c) A train leaves Grantham at quarter past 1 in the afternoon. It makes the same stops as the 06:31 train and takes the same time to travel between stops.

Complete the final column of the timetable to show this train.

3 A school bus makes this journey from Hall Lane to Moorfield Academy.

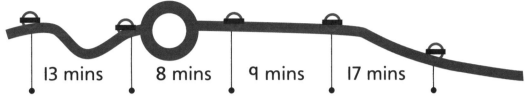

	13 mins	8 mins	9 mins	17 mins	
Hall Lane	Chapman Avenue	Wildshed Road	Station Road	Moorfield Academy

Complete the timetable to show:

• a bus that leaves Hall Lane at twenty minutes to 8 in the morning

• a bus that arrives at Moorfield Academy at twenty-five minutes to 4 in the afternoon.

	Bus 1	Bus 2
Hall Lane		
Chapman Avenue		
Wildshed Road		
Station Road		
Moorfield Academy		

I am going to have to work back in time for one of these buses!

Reflect

Why do you think timetables are written using 24-hour clock times? Think about the mistakes that could happen if they were not.

- _____
- _____
- _____

Date: _____

Problem solving – units of measure

1 **a)** Convert the measurements to find the totals.

This information uses different units! I think I am going to need to convert.

| 7,200 ml | | l l |
| 7,200 ml | + | l l |

7,200 ml + [＿＿] ml = [＿＿] ml

6·2 kg   2,000 g

[＿＿] g + [＿＿] g = [＿＿] g

b) In each of these examples, I converted the numbers by _____

_____ .

2 A length of string is 1·4 m long. An 80 cm long piece is cut from it.

What length of string is left in centimetres?

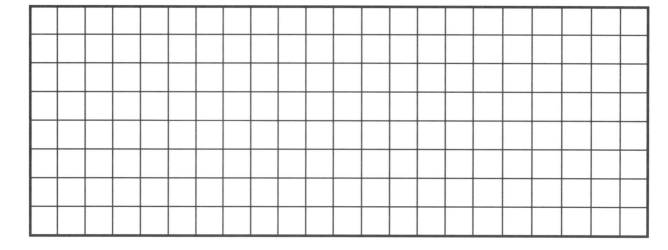

3 Show how you can find each answer using two different units.

a) $800 \text{ g} + \frac{1}{2} \text{ kg}$

$= 800 \text{ g} + \boxed{} \text{ g}$

$= \boxed{} \text{ g}$

$800 \text{ g} + \frac{1}{2} \text{ kg}$

$= \boxed{} \text{ kg} + \boxed{} \text{ kg}$

$= \boxed{} \text{ kg}$

b) $10 \cdot 5 \text{ cm} - 62 \text{ mm}$

$= 10 \cdot 5 \text{ cm} - \boxed{} \text{ cm}$

$= \boxed{} \text{ cm}$

$10 \cdot 5 \text{ cm} - 62 \text{ mm}$

$= \boxed{} \text{ mm} - 62 \text{ mm}$

$= \boxed{} \text{ mm}$

4 Put these shopping bags in order from lightest to heaviest.

Lightest _____ , _____ , _____ , _____ Heaviest

5 Richard makes some orange squash by mixing $\frac{1}{10}$ l of orange juice with 1 l of water in a jug.

CHALLENGE

He pours 300 ml of squash into a glass.

a) How many ml of squash does he have left in the jug? Show your working.

b) Richard pours the rest of the squash into 4 glasses equally. How much squash is in each glass?

Reflect

How would you write the total of 250 m and 0·6 km in metres?

Problem solving – units of measure ❷

 → Textbook 5C p208

1 A bag of coins has a mass of 2·7 kg. How many grams is this?

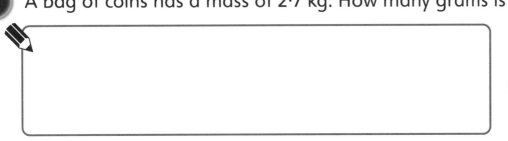

2·7 kg

2·7 kg is ☐ grams.

2 This ruler shows the distance in centimetres that a frog has jumped.

How many metres has it jumped?

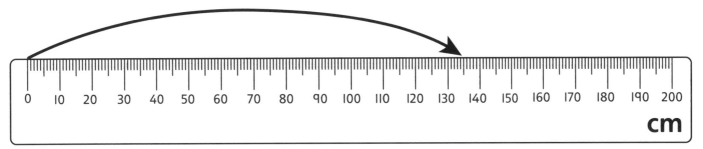

cm

The frog has jumped ☐ metres.

3 A teacup holds 150 ml. Zac empties three teacups of water into a measuring jug.

Mark the level of the water that is now in the jug.

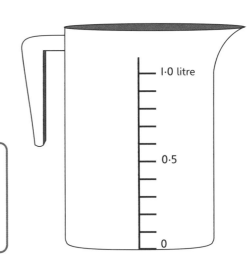

1·0 litre

0·5

0

155

4 A box of strawberries has a mass of 1·6 kg. It is shared equally among 10 people. How many grams of strawberries do they each get?

They get ☐ g each.

5 Ebo's mum wants to buy 4 yards of material to make a dress.

Shop A sells material for £1·50 per yard. Shop B sells the same material for £2 per metre.

Which shop is cheaper?

> I yard is approximately 90 cm.

Shop _____ is cheaper.

6 A net of 5 footballs has a mass of 2·8 kg in total.

The net itself has a mass of 800 g.

What mass does 1 football have in grams?

One football has a mass of ☐ g.

7 These photo frames are the same distance apart on a wall. Each photo frame is 20 cm wide. The total length of wall that the frames take up is 1·25 m.

CHALLENGE

What is the length of each space between the photos?

20 cm   20 cm   20 cm   20 cm

1·25 m

I need to decide whether to work in metres or centimetres.

The length of each space is ⬚ _____ .

Reflect

Olivia has a ball of string and a ruler that measures in inches.
She needs to cut a piece of string 1 m long. Explain how she can measure it.

Date: _____

End of unit check

My journal

→ Textbook 5C p212

My bottle holds 1·2 l of water. How many millilitres is this?

1 Explain how you would convert these measurements.

a) 1·2 l = [ ] ml

I know this because _____

_____

_____.

My train journey took 490 minutes. How many hours and minutes did it take?

b) 490 minutes = [ ] hours [ ] minutes

I know this because _____

_____

_____.

c) 60 inches = [ ] metres

I know this because _____

_____

_____.

How many metres are the same as 60 inches?

Power check

How do you feel about your work in this unit?

Power play

Play this game of three-in-a-row with a partner. You will need: different coloured counters, a dice and this railway timetable.

START						
Greenhill	06:42	10:02	13:22	16:42	20:02	23:22
Newton	06:57	10:17	13:37	16:57	20:17	23:37
Wood End	07:18	10:38	13:58	17:18	20:38	23:58
Amington	07:27	10:47	14:07	17:27	20:47	00:07
Ellwich	07:42	11:02	14:22	17:42	21:02	00:22
Garford	08:05	11:25	14:45	18:05	21:25	00:45

Put a counter on START.

Roll a dice. Move your counter that number of squares right. Roll the dice again. Move your counter that number of squares down.

Say a fact about the square you land on. For example, if you rolled a 3 and a 4, you could say: 'The twenty-two minutes past 1 train from Greenhill arrives at Amington at seven minutes past 2.'

If you and your partner agree this is a correct fact, leave your plastic counter on the square, if not remove your counter.

Take turns with your partner.

The winner is the first person to have three counters in a row.

> Try inventing your own game where your partner has to work out the time different trains take!

Date: _____

Cubic centimetres

1 What is the volume of each shape?

a)

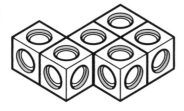

Volume = ☐ cm³

d)

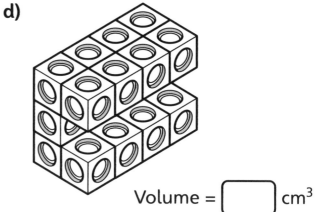

Volume = ☐ cm³

b)

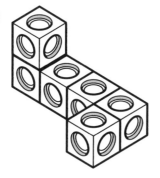

Volume = ☐ cm³

e)

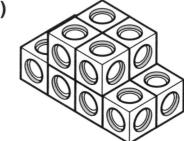

Volume = ☐ cm³

c)

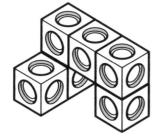

Volume = ☐ cm³

f)

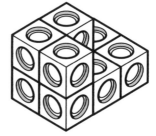

Volume = ☐ cm³

2 Match the shapes to the correct volume.

| 6 cm³ | 8 cm³ | 12 cm³ | 16 cm³ |

3

Richard

The volume of this 3D shape is 6 cm³.

Do you think Richard is correct? Explain your answer.

_____

_____

4 What is the volume of each of the following shapes?

A   B   C

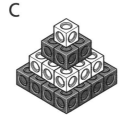

Shape	Volume
Shape A	5 cm³
Shape B	☐ cm³
Shape C	☐ _____

Explain to a partner how you got your answers.

5 Draw a copy of each cube on the isometric grid.

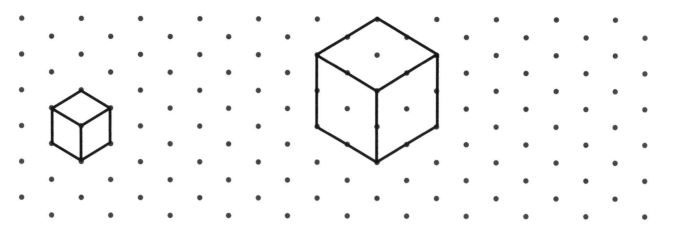

6 Max uses 4 cm³ cubes to make a 3D shape. Draw two different 3D shapes that each have a volume of 4 cm³.

CHALLENGE

Reflect

Explain what is meant by volume. How do you measure volume?

Date: _____

Compare volumes

1 Tick the shape in each set that has the greatest volume.

a)

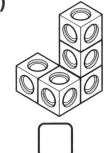

☐   ☐

b)

   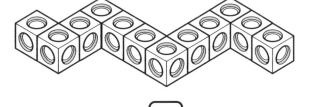   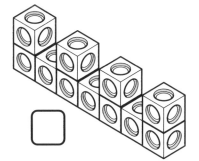

☐   ☐   ☐

c)

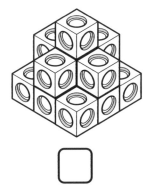   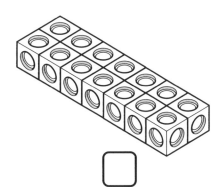

☐   ☐

d) Did you need to count all the cubes in each shape?

Explain your answer.

_____

_____

_____

Textbook 5C p220

2 Sort these shapes. List them from greatest to least volume.

A B C D

Greatest volume ⬜ , ⬜ , ⬜ , ⬜ Least volume

3 Match each shape to the correct person by writing their name under their shape.

My shape is half the volume of Bella's.

Amelia

My shape has more than 10 cm³ cubes.

Bella

My shape has a volume one third of Bella's shape.

Max

_____   _____   _____

4 Add cubes to shape A so that it has the same volume as shape B.

A

B

5 Aki makes a tower that has a volume of 15 cm³.

Emma makes a cuboid 4 cm long, 2 cm wide and 2 cm high.

Predict who has made the shape with the greatest volume.

I predict that _____ has made the shape with the

greatest volume because _____.

Now make each shape and check. Was your prediction correct?

_____

CHALLENGE

Reflect

Explain why two shapes that are made up of the same number of cubes can be different shapes but can have the same volume.

_____

_____

_____

165

Date: _____

Estimate volume

1. Ambika estimates the volume of each 3D shape by making it with cubes.

a)

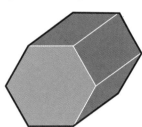

b)

Estimate of volume

= ☐ cm³

Estimate of volume

= ☐ cm³

2. Lexi builds some cubes to estimate the volume of her pencil.

Lexi says the volume of the pencil is 12 cm³.

How accurate do you think Lexi's estimate is? Explain your answer.

_____

_____

_____

166

3 Ebo has built this shape to estimate the volume of a 3D shape.

a) Tick the shape Ebo is estimating the volume of.

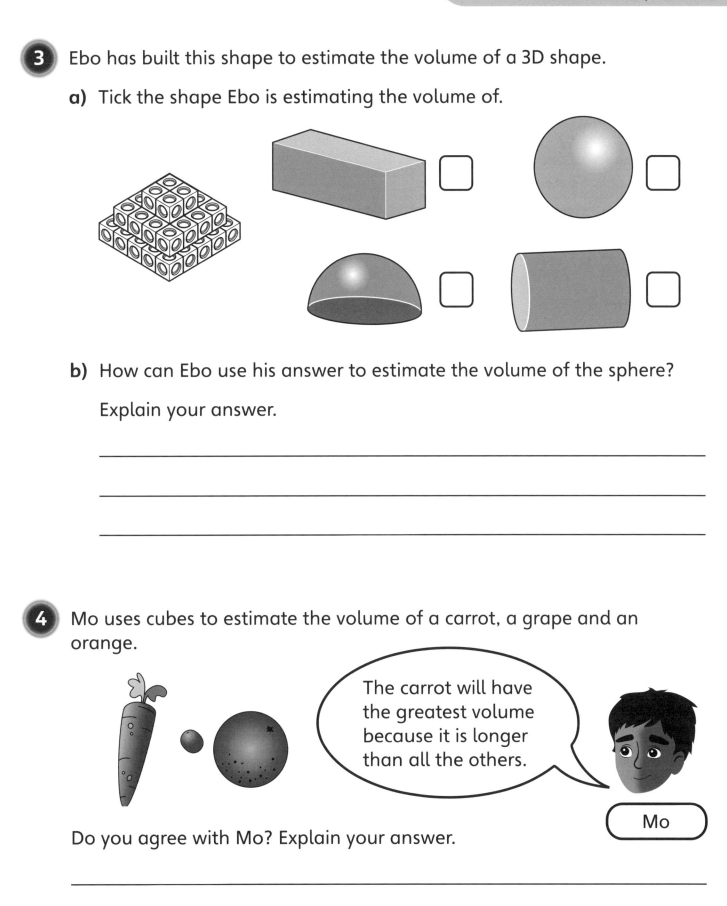

b) How can Ebo use his answer to estimate the volume of the sphere?

Explain your answer.

_____

_____

_____

4 Mo uses cubes to estimate the volume of a carrot, a grape and an orange.

The carrot will have the greatest volume because it is longer than all the others.

Mo

Do you agree with Mo? Explain your answer.

_____

_____

167

5 Estimate the volume of the following items you might find in your school.

Estimate:

☐ cm³

Estimate:

☐ cm³

Estimate:

☐ cm³

6 Complete the table with objects you might find in your classroom or at home.

CHALLENGE

Volume less than 10 cm³	Volume between 10 and 100 cm³	Volume between 100 and 1,000 cm³

Reflect

Explain how you could estimate the volume of your hand.

End of unit check

→ Textbook 5C p228

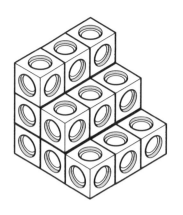

Explain two different ways to work out the volume of this shape.

Power puzzle

How many footballs do you think could fit into your classroom?

Think about how you can make the most accurate estimate possible.

Explain your strategy clearly. Use both diagrams and words.

Use your workings to estimate the total number of footballs that could fit into your entire school.

My power points

Put a tick against the topics you have learnt about. Show how confident you are with each one by giving it a number on a scale of 1 to 3.

1 = not at all confident;
2 = getting there;
3 = very confident

Unit 12

I have learnt how to …

☐ Measure all types of angles ☐

☐ Calculate angles ☐

☐ Recognise perpendicular and parallel lines ☐

☐ Reason with 3D shapes ☐

Unit 13

I have learnt how to …

☐ Read and plot coordinates ☐

☐ Translate shapes ☐

☐ Reflect shapes in vertical and horizontal lines ☐

Unit 14

I have learnt how to …

☐ Add and subtract decimals ☐

☐ Problem solve with decimals ☐

☐ Complete decimal sequences ☐

☐ Multiply by 10, 100 and 1,000 ☐

☐ Divide by 10, 100 and 1,000 ☐

Unit 15

I have learnt how to …

☐ Understand negative numbers

☐ Count through zero

☐ Compare and order negative numbers

☐ Find the difference between numbers

☐
☐
☐
☐

Unit 16

I have learnt how to …

☐ Convert units of length

☐ Understand imperial units of measure

☐ Understand timetables

☐ Problem solve with units of measure

☐
☐
☐
☐

Keep up the good work!

Notes

Squared paper

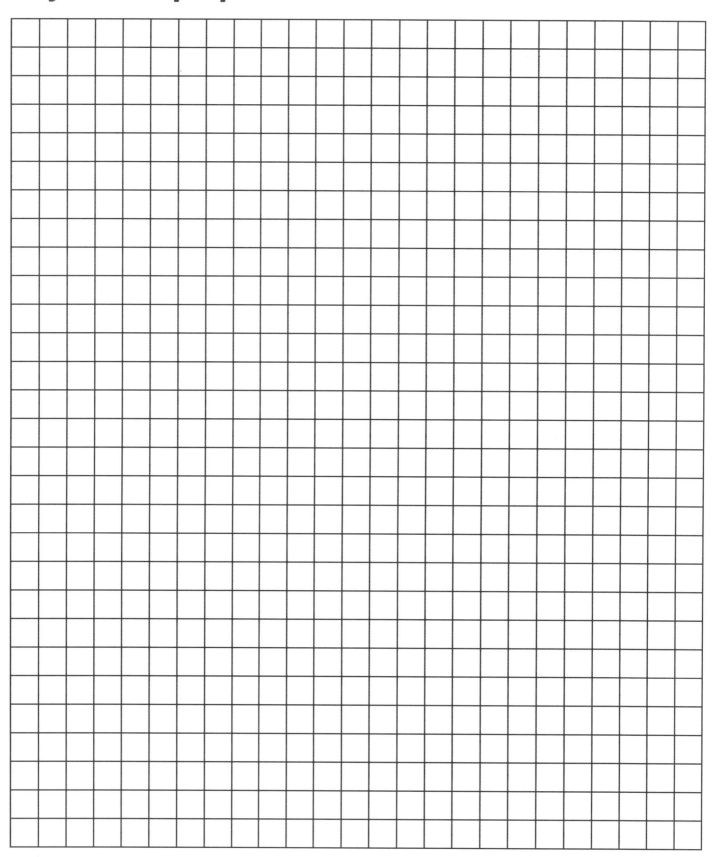

Squared paper

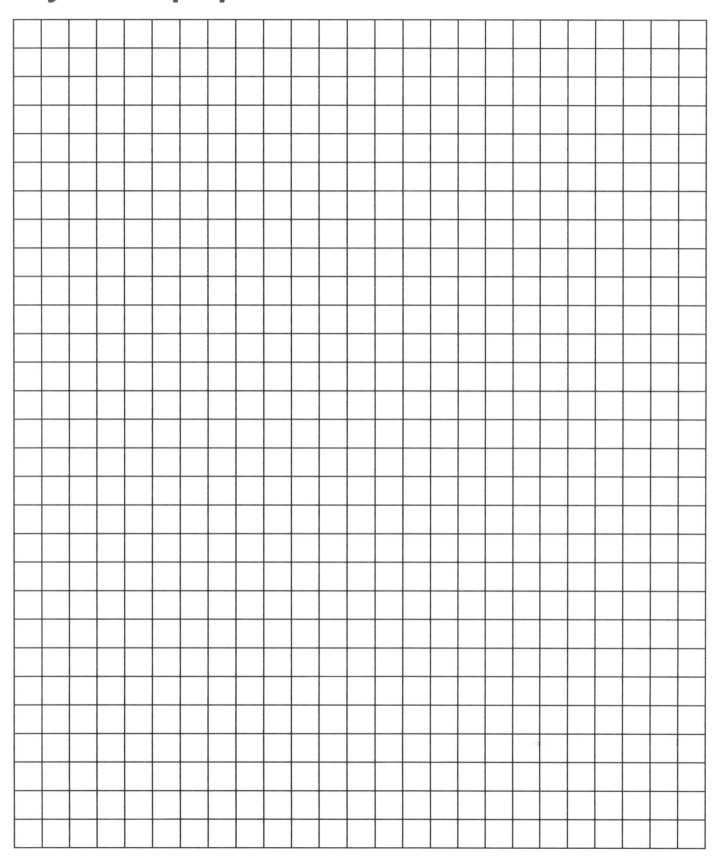

Published by Pearson Education Limited, 80 Strand, London, WC2R 0RL.

www.pearsonschools.co.uk

Text © Pearson Education Limited 2018, 2023
Edited by Pearson and Florence Production Ltd
First edition edited by Pearson, Little Grey Cells Publishing Services and Haremi Ltd
Designed and typeset by Pearson and PDQ Digital Media Solutions Ltd
First edition designed and typeset by Kamae Design
Original illustrations © Pearson Education Limited 2018, 2023
Illustrated by Laura Arias, John Batten, Fran and David Brylewski, Diego Diaz, Nigel Dobbyn and Nadene Naude at
Beehive Illustration; Emily Skinner at Graham-Cameron Illustration; and Kamae Design
Cover design by Pearson Education Ltd
Front and back cover illustrations by Diego Diaz and Nadene Naude at Beehive Illustration

Series editor: Tony Staneff
Lead author: Josh Lury
Consultants (first edition): Professor Liu Jian and Professor Zhang Dan

The rights of Tony Staneff and Josh Lury to be identified as authors of this work have been asserted by them in
accordance with the Copyright, Designs and Patents Act 1988.

First published 2018
This edition first published 2023

27 26 25 24 23
10 9 8 7 6 5 4 3 2 1

British Library Cataloguing in Publication Data
A catalogue record for this book is available from the British Library

ISBN 978 1 292 41963 3

Printed in the UK by Bell & Bain Ltd, Glasgow

For Power Maths resources go to
www.activelearnprimary.co.uk

Note from the publisher
Pearson has robust editorial processes, including answer and fact checks, to ensure the accuracy of the content in this
publication, and every effort is made to ensure this publication is free of errors. We are, however, only human, and
occasionally errors do occur. Pearson is not liable for any misunderstandings that arise as a result of errors in this
publication, but it is our priority to ensure that the content is accurate. If you spot an error, please do contact us at
resourcescorrections@pearson.com so we can make sure it is corrected.